HOMEOWNERS INSURANCE BASICS

WHAT YOU DON'T KNOW COULD COST YOU THOUSANDS

HON. ERIC DICK, ESQ.

Homeowners Insurance Basics

What You Don't Know Could Cost You Thousands

Author: Hon. Eric Dick, Esq.

Editor: Marc Cowart

ISBN: 979-8-89145-051-6

First Edition 2023

For more information about Eric and his practice, please visit:

www.DickLawFirm.com

For speaking requests or other inquiries, please phone

888-660-0088x700 or email **Eric@DickLawFirm.com**.

Disclaimer

Disclaimer: Although the author is a licensed attorney, the information contained in this book is for general informational purposes only and should not be considered legal advice. The content is provided "as is" without warranty of any kind, express or implied. The author and publisher make no representation or warranty as to the accuracy, completeness, or currency of the information contained in this book, and they shall not be liable for any damages whatsoever, including but not limited to special, consequential, or incidental damages, arising out of or in connection with the use or reliance upon any information contained herein. Readers are strongly advised to consult with a licensed attorney for specific legal advice related to their individual circumstances.

DEDICATION

This book is dedicated to the pillars of my life—my incredible wife Danielle, our beautiful daughters Grace and Caroline, and our precious little Liam. You have been my constant support, my inspiration, and the driving force behind everything I do.

Danielle, your unwavering love and belief in me have been my guiding light. You've been my partner, my confidante, and my rock. Your strength, grace, and unwavering support have pushed me to achieve more than I ever thought possible.

Grace and Caroline, you two are my greatest blessings. Your laughter, curiosity, and boundless energy fill our home with joy. Watching you grow and flourish has been the most rewarding experience of my life. You inspire me to dream big and to embrace the wonders of the world.

And Liam, my little bundle of joy, you have brought a new level of happiness and love to our family. Your innocent smile and infectious giggles light up our lives in ways we never imagined.

To my family, you have sacrificed and stood by my side through the late nights, the long hours, and the ups and downs of this journey. Your unwavering patience and understanding have allowed me to pursue my passions and dreams.

This book is a testament to the love, dedication, and support you have showered upon me. It is a small token of my gratitude for being my biggest cheerleaders and for inspiring me to reach for the stars.

May this dedication serve as a reminder of the deep love and appreciation I have for each one of you. Together, we are a team, and with you by my side, I know there is no limit to what we can achieve.

With all my love,

Eric

CONTENTS

CHAPTER ONE
WHAT IS HOMEOWNERS INSURANCE?

A (Very) Brief History of Homeowners Insurance

Insurance is a concept almost as old as history itself. It did not take humans long to learn that life came with risk, so we began thinking of ways to lessen the risk or avoid it. And if disaster struck, we looked for the fairest and most convenient way to rebuild afterward.

There was a time when homeowners "insurance" existed by virtue of the fact that we lived in communities. Being a member of a group, tribe, clan, or family meant that everyone looked out for each other. If Nathan's house burned, everyone would come together to help him rebuild and restock. Of course, it was part of the unspoken agreement that Nathan, in turn, would do the same if his neighbor Opie's home was destroyed. This was the point of living in groups – together is better than alone. Naturally, if Opie or Nathan were lazy members who refused to help, their "insurance" policy might be canceled by group decision. Membership in society comes with duties as well as rewards.

Modern homeowners insurance found its beginnings in the Great Fire of London in 1666. In that disaster, 13,000 homes were lost. A community can come together to rebuild one home. 13,000 is another matter entirely. Sir Christopher Wren, the premier architect of the time, attempted to redesign London afterward (unsuccessfully, since the people were not willing to wait for plans to be approved before rebuilding their homes) and proposed the idea of an Insurance Office. He expressed the opinion that property insurance had changed "from a matter of convenience into one of urgency." In 1681, economist Nicholas Barbon and his associates established the "Insurance Office for Houses," which was backed by the Royal Exchange. It opened a business with 5,000 brick-and-frame homes insured.

By the 18th Century, our resourceful Nathan would have certainly signed up for a fire insurance contract for his own home. But which one would he choose? There were many to pick from, like the Hand in Hand Fire & Life Insurance Society and the Sun Fire Office. Nathan's biggest problem would have been that insurance companies provided their own firefighters, and regardless of how close they might be when Nathan's house went up in flames, they were not keen on offering those firefighting services to Nathan, who had chosen to go with a different company. Nathan's house burned down, leading him and others to understand that making firefighting a "member's only" service was not a great idea, since fire tends to spread.

They agreed upon a solution in which all the insurance companies would fund and supply equipment to a municipal authority that stationed fire prevention assets and firefighters equally around the same area.

In the United States, the first insurance company that underwrote fire insurance was formed in Charles Town, South Carolina in 1732. Benjamin Franklin helped to popularize and standardize the practice of insurance, particularly property insurance, to reduce risk and loss in the form of perpetual insurance. He wisely founded the Philadelphia Contributionship for the Insurance of Houses from Loss by Fire in 1752. He and his company spread fire-safety awareness and even refused to insure certain buildings where the risk was too great.

However, the Federal government did not mandate any form of insurance upon the nation as a whole until the passage of the Social Security Act in 1935. That new program expanded the concept and acceptance of insurance. Insurance experienced its first boom market after World War II, with VA Home Loan programs that normalized the idea that veterans could afford a house. The Federal government underwrote these mortgages and included an insurance clause as a means of protecting any interested banks and lending institutions against avoidable losses.[1]

Until recent history, fire was the most likely way Nathan, Opie, or anyone else could lose their home. Safety regulations, the Fire Prevention Act and construction improvements gave us a society in which your home is actually more likely to be damaged by wind and hail (about 40% of claims), with the chance for fire or lightning damage coming in second (about 35% of claims).

Now that we have covered a bit of history let's look at the present.

Where We Are Now

If you are like most people, your home is your most valuable asset. What's more, it's essential— life gets rough without a place to lay your head at night—and it only makes

1 Prudential Insurance Company of America, ed. *The Documentary History of Insurance, 1000 B. C.-1875 A. D.* (1915)

sense to protect your home with a good insurance policy. The world is unpredictable, and a storm, crime, or accident could ruin your investment – and your stability and safety – if you are not properly insured. This same insurance can even help you cope with the difficulties of recovering from such an event.

Of course, I hope you never lose your home and have to go through a complete home replacement or rebuilding. That's really an extreme example. Much of the time, a homeowners policy is there to protect you from more common occurrences.

While this book will focus on homeowners insurance policies specified in the state of Texas, some aspects of these policies are true throughout the United States.

We'll start with the basics! Let's begin with what homeowners insurance is and why you need it. Chances are that you already know the answer to these questions, and you picked up this book because you have a specific question about a policy you have, a policy that you want to buy, a claim that you want to make, or perhaps even one that you are having trouble making. Don't worry, we'll cover all of these subjects. Understanding the basics of homeowners insurance will make everything easier as we move along.

Three Purposes of Coverage

Homeowners insurance comes into play in three different scenarios:

Damage or destruction to the house's interior and exterior. When your house becomes damaged, the policy will pay for the cost to repair, or even rebuild, the home. This portion of the policy covers damage caused by fires, storms, or vandalism, for example—but usually not floods, earthquakes, or any damage caused by ordinary use, the passage of time, or poor home construction choices you might make! Policies are customizable. We will cover many more details about this aspect to talk about extras like adding riders to your policy or insuring outbuildings like sheds or garages.

Theft or loss of possessions. Most of a home's contents are covered by a homeowners insurance policy. Furniture, appliances, clothing, and electronics, for example, are all replaceable if a peril covered by your policy destroys them. Typically, contents are covered for 50 to 70 percent of your home structure (dwelling) coverage. That means if your house is covered for $400,000, you will likely have somewhere between $200,000 and $280,000 coverage for your possessions. We'll go into this more later because there are a few extras you might want to include, such as "off-premises" coverage or extra measures to take if you have particularly valuable possessions like collector's items, jewelry, or art.

Personal liability in case of injury or damages. This is the insurance coverage that protects you from lawsuits filed by people injured on your property. Say Uncle Jody falls down the stairs and breaks a hip – your homeowner's insurance pays a portion of his medical expenses. There are some interesting ways that this aspect of your policy can be used to protect you, even outside your home—such as if you inadvertently cause damage to someone else's property—and we'll definitely go into more detail about those.

Cash Value vs. Replacement Cost

There are three levels of coverage, from least expensive to most: **Actual Cash Value, Replacement Cost,** and **Guaranteed Replacement Cost** (sometimes also called **Extended Replacement Cost**). As you have probably guessed, the least expensive option is also the one that provides the least amount of coverage. The difference between the coverages are as follows:

Actual Cash Value: This type of policy covers the cost of your house and your belongings at their *current* value. In other words, it is not the price you paid but the item's value at the time of loss. That means a TV you bought for $1,000 five years ago may only be worth $500 now, so your insurance would only compensate you $500 for its loss.

In most cases, the actual structure of your home will be covered at Replacement Cost (see below), but your personal property is most likely covered at Actual Cash Value.

Replacement Cost: This policy covers the actual cash value of your home *without* taking depreciation into consideration.

Extended Replacement Cost and Guaranteed Replacement Cost: This is a comprehensive policy that pays for the replacement of your home's structure, even if that replacement exceeds your policy limits. Extended Replacement Cost has a cap of 20 to 25 percent higher than policy limits. Guaranteed Replacement Costs have no cap limit and are more expensive policies, obviously. These policies protect you against rises in replacement costs and construction prices.

Standardized Homeowners Insurance Forms

Since 1984, The United States insurance industry has had eight standardized forms that offer varying levels of protection. The protection levels depend on the type of residence and the homeowner's need. In most jurisdictions, the same standard homeowners insurance forms are used, but even if your jurisdiction differs, your insurance broker should be able to find you the equivalent policy. Most jurisdictions no longer use Forms HO-1 or HO-7.

1. **HO-1, Basic Form**
   a. Covers only 10 of the 16 perils. This policy will not cover falling objects or the weight of ice damage.
   b. Because the policy is so limited, it is seldom offered by modern insurance companies.
   c. Only available to the owner/occupant of a one-to-four-family dwelling that is used for private residential purposes (with allowances for home offices, for example).
2. **HO-2, Broad Form**
   a. Largely like the HO-1.
   b. However, provides somewhat "broader" coverage.
   c. Only available to the owner/occupant of a one-to-four-family dwelling that is used for private residential purposes (with allowances for home offices, for example).
3. **HO-3, Special Form**
   a. Most common homeowners insurance policy form.

b. Offers "open peril" coverage for your dwelling, meaning that it will help pay for repairs to damage to your dwelling caused by a peril unless that peril is *excluded* from your policy documents.

c. Offers "named peril" coverage for personal property, which will repair or replace belongings damaged by peril – unless that peril is excluded in your policy documents.

d. Only available to the owner/occupant of a one-to-four-family dwelling that is used for private residential purposes (with allowances for home offices, for example).

4. **H-04, Contents Broad Form**

   a. This is the standard RENTERS insurance policy.

   b. Protects renter's personal belongings from 16 perils.

   c. Does NOT cover damage to the rental unit. (A separate, landlord-owned insurance policy covers this).

   d. Can also be used in the situation of a home where more than four families live.

   e. Co-operative members can fill out an H-04 or an H-06.

5. **H-05, Comprehensive Form**

   a. This type of home insurance is written on an "open perils" basis, which means it covers damage to your home or personal property as long as its cause is not listed on the exclusions in the policy.

b. Better coverage but is possibly more costly than an HO-3 policy. This is because, with an HO-5, your personal property is also included under "open perils" protection rather than limiting it to the "named perils" as in the HO-3 policy.

6. **H-06, Unit Owners Form**

    a. This form is for Condominium or Co-operative Insurance.

    b. Includes what is called "walls-in" coverage, meaning it protects the walls, floors, and ceilings against 16 perils.

    c. Also protects the condo owner's belongings.

    d. A separate policy protects the condominium's common areas and the building, usually maintained by the condominium association.

    e. The condominium unit also has a minimum premium of $1,000 covering the following property:

        i. Changes, appliances, fixtures, and upgrades are part of the residence premises, such as appliances, carpets, extra kitchen cabinets, and wallpaper.

        ii. Actual property pertains solely to residence premises, such as a patio, balcony, or patio trees or shrubs.

        iii. Property that could be the insured's responsibility under the condominium owners' agreement, such as fixtures or interior partitions.

iv. Structures owned exclusively by the insured, other than the condominium unit at the condominium site, such as a private garage or fence.

f. Co-operative members can fill out an H-04 or an H-06.

7. **H-07, Mobile Home**

    a. This is the mobile home insurance policy.

    b. A modified version of the H-02 policy.

8. **H-08, Modified Coverage Form**

    a. This form protects older homes. Older or historic homes (about 40 years and older) sometimes do not qualify for H-03 coverage because they have original wiring or plumbing. Rebuilding older homes can be considerably more expensive due to changing codes and unconventional building methods or resources.

    b. Eligibility requirements are less stringent than in other forms, but the coverage is less extensive.

    c. Covers up to ten perils only and does not include things such as water or electricity damage due to original wiring/plumbing or damages like cracking, burning, or bulging in the structure.

    d. Covered damage is paid on actual cash value rather than replacement cost (pays the cost of the item minus depreciation).

    e. Homes that are historically registered or landmark-registered normally have this type of policy.

f. Only available to the owner/occupant of a one-to-four-family dwelling that is used for private residential purposes (with allowances for home offices, for example).

Sections of the Homeowners Insurance Policy

Each of the insurance policy types listed above contains two sections:

- Section I - is devoted to coverage of the property.
- Section II - is devoted to liability and medical coverage.

Let's break these sections into their parts and components.

Section I Coverages

Under Section I, you may find four types of coverage labeled A, B, C, and D. Each section covers a different aspect of protection. Note that not all policies contain all four types of coverage. For example, Form H-04 (the renter's policy) does not include Coverage A (protection on the dwelling) because that is not the responsibility of the renter.

The policy limits of each section are *usually* a percentage of the total amount for which your house is insured, and we'll provide that "most common" percentage. Remember, though, that in almost every case, these percentages can be adjusted based on need.

Coverage A	Protection on the dwelling itself.

Coverage B	Protection to other structures, normally equal to 10 percent of the amount of insurance on the dwelling.
Coverage C	Protection on personal property (the contents of your house). The limits under Coverage C are usually 50 percent of the dwelling's insured amount.
Coverage D	Protection for "loss of use," which means that if you "lose the use" of your house, the expenses incurred while it is being repaired are covered. The typical limit is 30 percent of the dwelling's insured amount.

Section II Coverages

Liability coverage protects you from a variety of damages or injuries that could be incurred either on your property, or elsewhere if the fault lies with you or with someone or something for which you are responsible. For example, if you inadvertently cause injury to another person by trampling on their foot in your swan dive to grab the homerun baseball at Minute Maid Park, if your daughter breaks the neighbor's plate glass window when she pitches that same baseball clean through it – good arm on that girl – or if your dog chases that baseball down the street and bites someone on the way, liability coverage can provide protection. Liability coverage under Section II is the same on every policy type – all policies will contain both Coverage E and F.

Coverage E	Provides personal liability protection. This covers damages that the insured is legally obligated to pay because of bodily injury or property damage. "Damages" in this case means pretty much anything except medical, such as the cost of repairs or lost wages. This also includes providing a defense for you if one is needed, like if a civil case is filed in court.
Coverage F	Provides medical payments (to others). This pays medical expenses incurred within three years of the cause of bodily injury. So, if your friend is hurt in your house or yard or the ways adjoining them, hurt by your own activities (like when you stomped his foot at the baseball game), hurt by the actions of anyone in your care (your daughter is still hurling that baseball like a champ), or any animal in your care (your dog, once more…), then his medical expenses are covered. Now, here's the catch: this coverage does not apply to *you*, the insured. If your dog bites you, tough luck, and if you get in the way of your daughter's fierce pitch, better duck. Sometimes this is called "guest medical" because it applies only to people who *don't* live with you.

There are a number of exclusions to personal liability coverage, more than we want to cover in this "basics" chapter. But this exclusion is pretty stable across the board: if the injury or damage is sustained because of an *intentional* or *illegal* activity, homeowners insurance will not provide protection.

Definition of Peril in the Homeowners Insurance Policy

"Peril" means an event that could cause damage to your home or your possessions. The perils covered by a homeowners insurance policy are listed within the policy. There are sixteen named perils covered in insurance, but not every policy covers every peril – and of course, we will be covering what those perils are and to what extent they are covered in Chapter Three. If you have a current policy, you should check it to learn which perils are, and which are not, covered within.

An "Open-peril policy" means that *you are covered unless a specific peril is excluded in your policy.*

A "Named-peril policy" means that *you are covered only for the perils listed in your policy.*

These sound like almost the same thing, don't they? Let's examine the difference with a simple example.

Opie and Nathan are homeowners who live next door to each other; Opie has an open-peril policy and Nathan has a named-peril policy. Opie's policy says that he is covered for all perils excluding floods and earthquakes, so his policy is *open* to all other perils. Nathan's policy says that he is covered for the perils of fire, smoke, falling objects, vandalism, theft, and riots, so his policy *names* the perils it covers.

Their neighborhood is about to have a very bad week. On Monday, a fire rages through the neighborhood foliage, causing severe smoke damage to the homes. Luckily, both Opie and Nathan are covered: Opie's policy doesn't exclude smoke damage, and Nathan's policy names it.

But, oh no! On Tuesday, a tornado tears apart everyone's roof and siding. Opie is still covered; windstorms are not excluded on his policy. But Nathan is in trouble because windstorms are not named in his.

On Wednesday, an earthquake shakes the neighborhood to the ground. Now, both homeowners are in the same boat: Opie's policy excludes earthquakes, and Nathan's does not name earthquakes as a coverage.

Therefore, on Thursday, both men begin actively looking for homes in a less dangerous neighborhood.

Homeowners insurance policies generally recognize far more perils than poor Nathan's, but you get the idea.

Basic, Broad Form, and Special Coverage

Property insurance has three levels of coverage against perils:

Basic Coverage: This is sometimes referred to as "Standard Coverage." As the name suggests, this level provides the "basic"—or in other words, a minimum—level of protection against fire, theft, and vandalism.

Broad Form Coverage: This is basic coverage that has been extended to include a number of additional named perils.

Special Coverage: This is the name for protection on an open-peril basis.

Most homeowners policies (excluding HO-8, because it is designed for older homes) fall under the Broad Form or Special Coverage categories, and of course, the HO-4 (renters policy) applies only to the contents of the dwelling.

Bases – and Basics – Covered

This chapter has been a quick and simple summary of the common types, parts, and purposes of a homeowners insurance policy. But, if everything about insurance was quick and simple, there wouldn't need to be a book! There is a great deal of variation to be found within individual insurance policies, so the best way to know for certain what is covered is to go straight to the source: the policy itself. I hope that this chapter has given you the tools you need to get the most benefit out of the rest of this book.

CHAPTER TWO

BUYING A POLICY: HOW TO AND HOW MUCH

Do I *have* to have homeowners insurance?

Let's be honest – most of us obtain a homeowners insurance policy because our mortgage company requires us to do so. We are so busy closing on a home, moving in, and finally enjoying our purchase that we may not even consider the coverage we quickly purchased from the first or second company we called up. All homeowners insurance is basically the same, right? Or, at least, it is until something happens—and then, you discover that not all insurance companies and not all policies are created equal.

One thing your mortgage lender will get right is ensuring that you have a policy that covers the cost of replacing the structure of your home. The home is the collateral for the loan they are extending to you, and they want it well-protected. However, they do not care nearly so much for your possessions or your liability coverage, and if you never paid much attention, you probably have cookie-cutter policy limits. Are these sufficient to protect you and your property?

On the other hand, you may not have a mortgage. Unlike automobile insurance, there is no legal requirement that you have homeowners insurance in Texas. In fact, many Texas homeowners who are not required to have insurance, *don't,* despite the fact that they live in areas susceptible to storm damage. The Texas Real Estate Research Center conducted a study after the devastating winter storm Uri in February of 2021. This mercilessly frigid storm resulted in an estimated $130 billion in damages, while leaving a surprising number of non-insured homeowners carrying the cost of repairs on their own. Investigation of this situation confirmed that in metro areas, about one-in-ten homes are uninsured, and in non-metro areas, a whopping one out of four of homes are uninsured. In most cases, the uninsured homes were not under mortgage; only about four percent of mortgaged homes were uninsured. (Remember – most mortgage lenders will require proof of insurance before allowing a loan to close.)[2]

Your home is likely your most valuable possession. Keeping an insurance policy on it is simply the smart thing to do. One angry day from Mother Nature could decimate your investment, or one unexpected injury on your property could mean big trouble for you and your assets if you're not protected.

Now, that's easy to say – but suppose you cannot afford a policy. The study above confirms that the majority of uninsured homes belonged to lower-income households. If the cost of homeowners insurance seems prohibitive, I will soon have some advice for you on how to spend less and still obtain good coverage. And let's face it – not having insurance could end up costing you *much* more than paying for a policy.

---

2 Recenter.tamu.edu/articles/tierra-grande/storm-warning-2310

Even if you do not own your property, you can purchase a renters insurance policy which will provide protection for your possessions and for liability – something I highly recommend.

I don't know anyone who just *loves* making insurance payments. It can certainly feel like a big chunk of money going away for no clear-cut benefit…until something goes haywire, someone takes a fall, or the weather turns nasty. If someday you need to file a claim, you will be extremely glad that you've maintained your policy. And if you never need to file a claim, you're living a charmed life! That sounds like a win-win.

In this chapter, we'll go over some common questions and issues about purchasing a policy.

How much do I actually need?

The following levels of homeowners insurance coverage are recommended[3]:

Dwelling Coverage: You should have coverage equal to your home's replacement cost. Base this on *rebuilding* costs, not your home's price. Considerations for the cost of rebuilding include the location and condition of your house and the construction/repair prices in your region. Occasionally, you should check your home coverage to ensure that it does not fall below the cost of repairing your home. If it drops below 80-percent of your home's full replacement cost, your insurance provider will reduce the sum it will pay on a claim.

Personal Property Coverage: You should have coverage sufficient to replace your belongings. This in-

3 www.investopedia.com/how-much-homeowners-insurance-do-i-need-4783621

cludes everything in your house that is not a part of the house. Later in this book, we will discuss how to best assess the value of your belongings. In a typical policy, personal property limits will be a percentage of your dwelling coverage. You will need to investigate additional coverage if you own valuable items, art, or collectibles.

Additional Living Expenses: You should have 10-to-30-percent of your dwelling coverage. This is the money that takes care of you if you are displaced. Some costs included are hotels, dining, laundry, furniture rental, storage for your belongings, and pet boarding. Commonly, insurance policies calculate this at 20-percent of the dwelling coverage. Consider your circumstances: if your family is larger, it is a good idea to consider higher policy limits.

Liability Coverage: You should have as much of this as you can afford. I know that's not the most helpful answer, but it is certainly helpful coverage. Most homeowners insurance policies automatically have $100,000 in liability coverage. Bumping that up to $300,000 is smart and bumping it up even higher is even smarter.

The five most common liability claims filed by homeowners are:

1. Dog bites – it happens. We love dogs, but they do bite. Even the best-behaved dog in the world can bite if it thinks it is protecting you.

2. Home Accidents – and this even includes injuries to people who were not invited. That door-to-door salesperson can sue you after breaking an ankle on your porch.

3. Falling trees – age, storms, disease, and pests, just to name a few things, can cause unexpected breakage in trees. If a tree falls in the forest and no one is around to hear it, well… no problem for you. If it falls from your yard onto your neighbor's roof or car, then you are liable for their damages.

4. Intoxicated guests – if someone becomes intoxicated on your property, you can be held liable for damage they do to other people or property. That's a scary thought!

5. Injured Domestic Workers – you can also be held liable for anyone hurt while working for you, such as anyone who is cutting your grass, cleaning your house, or fixing your sink.

Here's a little more bad news: it's possible that if medical expenses and damages for these incidents exceed your policy limits, you could be held accountable for the remainder. So, having extra liability coverage is a very, very good idea.

What about an umbrella insurance policy?

An umbrella insurance policy helps ensure that you never face the situation that we just mentioned: your policy has reached its limits and you are left holding the bag for the remaining damages. Umbrella policies are just for liability coverage, so they don't pay for damages to your home or injuries sustained by *you* or your dependents. Such policies are relatively inexpensive and, if you can afford one, it's not a bad idea. We live in a highly litigious society – people love to sue each other – and sometimes, accidents or incidents can spiral into expensive damages, and juries often reward verdicts far in excess of policy limits.

One factor to consider is how likely you are to be sued. We can never know what the future holds, but some people are targeted more often than others, such as if you are wealthy (or perceived to be wealthy), a public figure, or both. Not a celebrity? If you own many properties or have a lot of teenage drivers in the house, an umbrella policy might be a wise consideration.

A possible problem with an umbrella insurance policy is that it will probably require you to have maximum coverages on your homeowners insurance and automobile insurance first; this is because the umbrella policy would expect that primary insurance to pay first and pay up to its limits before the umbrella policy would activate.

Another option for increased liability coverage is that of ***endorsements***, which allow you to increase liability limits beyond what is ordinary. It is not quite the coverage of an umbrella policy, but it's far better than being left holding the bag.

What determines the price of a policy?

Like most insurance policies, prices will vary depending on the value of the item being insured, but also in that item's circumstances. It will probably cost more to ensure a Porsche than a Honda Civic, but the insurance company doesn't ignore the fact that the Porsche owner lives in Boise, is 55 years old, and has never had an accident, whereas the Honda's owner lives in L.A., is 22 years old, and has had four speeding tickets and two accidents in the last three years. Homeowners insurance premiums consider both the obvious and the not-so-obvious factors.Your premium can vary depending on:

- The home's size.
- The home's location.
- The home's age and condition.
- The home's building materials. It's true! Brick or masonry homes typically have lower premiums than wood-framed homes because they are wind and fire resistant.
- The home's history and the history of other homes in the area.
- The home's proximity to fire protection services and the availability of fire safety facilities in the neighborhood.
- The amount of personal property.
- The insurance company.
- The deductibles you agree to.
- Your credit history. (A poor credit history can raise your rates!)
- Your history of alleging damages or liability in other homes.
- The presence or lack of safety equipment in the house: smoke alarms, sprinkler systems, burglar alarms, door bolts, window protection devices. (Having these things is likely to lower your premiums.)
- The presence of a wood furnace or wood stove (potential fire hazards).
- The presence of a swimming pool, trampoline, or playscape (potentially injurious items).

- Your ownership of a certain type of dog that might be considered aggressive – such as German Shepherds, Chow Chows, or Pitbulls.

Unfortunately, homeowners insurance in Texas is the fifth most costly in the United States. Texas's average home insurance premium for the coverage standard of a $300,000 dwelling is $3,429, which is 49-percent higher than the national average of $2,305. One contributing factor to these costs is the extensive lobbying from the insurance industry. In 2020, Texans for Lawsuit Reform raised close to $17 million to influence the Texas government for laws more favorable to insurance companies. Lobbying efforts led to the Texas Department of Insurance turning a blind eye to insurance companies that were price-gouging consumers.

Insurance Required by Lenders

Mortgage companies (lenders) require that the home is insured before the loan is closed. It is important to them, so they will definitely let you know prior to closing exactly what they require. Then, the mortgage company will sometimes require special, additional insurance, particularly if the home you are buying is in a high-risk area.

Some of the more common additional insurance requirements, as well as their annual premium averages, in Texas[4] are:

1. **Flood insurance**. We'll discuss this further in Chapter Three, but a standard homeowners insurance policy does not cover flood damage. However, if you are buying a home in a high-risk flooding zone, it's quite likely that your mortgage company will want you to have

4 https://www.valuepenguin.com

flood insurance. Private insurers offer this protection at an additional charge; another option to consider is the National Flood Insurance Program (NFIP). The national average cost of flood insurance annually is $700, but if you live in a coastal area or on a riverfront, that cost might be much higher. On the bright side, the average cost in Texas is $618, almost 16-percent below that national average.

2. **Windstorm insurance**. Most of the time, windstorm damage is covered under insurance policies. Nevertheless, if a home is located in Tornado Alley or in an area regularly struck by hurricanes, insurance policies might exclude coverage, forcing you to purchase a separate windstorm policy. This type of insurance often has a percentage deductible. The average premium for windstorm insurance in Texas is about $1,600 per year. *Note: if you have been rejected for windstorm insurance by your regular insurance company, but you still want a policy, you can purchase a policy from the Texas Windstorm Insurance Association (TWIA).* Just remember that windstorm insurance doesn't cover damages caused by *water* that was blown into your home by that windstorm. A separate flood insurance policy will have to be purchased.

3. **Earthquake insurance**. As is the case with flood insurance, most standard policies don't cover earthquakes. So, once more, if you are buying a home in a zone that is high-risk for earthquakes, additional insurance may be required. Though our state does experience tectonic plate movement, seismic activity in Texas is usually not severe enough to cause damage, so this will be a less-frequent requirement. Typically, this type of insurance also has a percentage deductible, and these can be

rather high, up to 25-percent, meaning that damages of $100,000 could come bearing a $25,000 deductible.

4. **Water Backup coverage.** This protects a home from water damage due to overflowing drains or sewers and may be a requirement in neighborhoods with old sewer systems or areas where this problem has occurred frequently.

Your lender must be listed, along with you, as a payee for losses. This means that if you file a claim, the check will be made payable to both you and the mortgage company. The lender wants to ensure that the insurance money is spent on home repairs or replacement.

The lender will include a mortgage clause indicating that if your insurance company elects to cancel your homeowners coverage (due to your nonpayment, for example), the insurance company has to notify the lender in writing, 30 days in advance. This will allow the lender to obtain new insurance – at *your* expense. Which leads us to…

Force-placed coverage is quite expensive and will be required by your lender if you let your homeowners insurance policy lapse, or it is cancelled for any reason, and you don't obtain a new policy before it does. Here is the simple truth: you *must* pay for homeowners insurance on a mortgaged home, and one way or another, your lender will make sure that you do so. It is their right for lending you the money to purchase the home. It is best to pay your premiums on time and avoid the much more expensive alternative.

Some mortgage companies will allow you to add the cost of your homeowners insurance premiums into your monthly mortgage payment. This will increase your total monthly payment amount, of course, but it's one way to make sure the policy stays in effect, and it lessens the burden by letting you take care of two payments with one check – just remember to make your house payments regularly and on time!

What should I look for in a policy?

Based on our years of experience dealing with insurance claims, I have formed several recommendations for purchasing a homeowners insurance policy:

- Purchase a comprehensive policy that includes fire, windstorm, sudden and accidental water discharge, etc.
- Ideally, property insurance caps should be focused on the expense to repair the house. Periodically review your property tax appraisal evaluations to ensure that your policy keeps pace with leaps in value. Find out if construction costs are higher than average in your region.
- Purchase a policy that covers the *replacement* cost to your house, rather than the cash value. (We discussed the difference in Chapter One.) A replacement cash value homeowners insurance is more costly, but it pays out enough to restore or repair destroyed properties.
- Focus on the policy terms and conditions instead of the brand name.
- Buy low, *fixed* deductibles if possible, as opposed to a percentage deductible, which is likely to be much higher. If your home is insured at $300,000 and you have a one percent deductible, that amounts to a $3,000 deductible each time you file a claim.

How can I get a lower premium?

In all honesty, homeowners insurance is a must if you have a mortgage, and an extremely good idea even if you don't. You are going to pay for it, so why not get the best deal you can find? Here are some tips on how to lower your premiums.

1. Shop around. That is absolutely the first and best rule to making sure you are getting the most affordable rates for what you need. Shopping for insurance isn't most people's idea of a hot night out. However, if you don't do a little side-by-side comparison, you're likely to end up paying a lot more than you need to.

2. Generally, it's recommended to get quotes from several different insurers. Be certain when making comparisons that you are actually comparing the same types of policies, deductibles, and limits of coverage.

3. Add security features to your house, like an alarm system.

4. Increase your disaster resistance. Check with your insurance company representative first, but sometimes reinforcing roofs or framework, or modernizing your heating/plumbing systems can result in savings.

5. Hire an independent insurance agent to find and design your policy.

6. Save significant money by avoiding big-name insurance companies. Their prices are higher because they lobby congress and pay for slick, expensive television campaigns.

7. Accepting higher deductibles is certainly a way to lower your premiums, but I don't recommend it. High deductibles really defeat the whole purpose of insurance. The smarter move is to shop around for the best rates.

8. Buy auto and homeowners policies from the same company. Companies often reduce premiums significantly if you have two or more policies with them. Just don't assume it is the best option until you have confirmed that you can't get better savings by buying policies from someone else.

9. Staying with the same company for many years can qualify you for special premium discounts.

10. Check into other discounts available. It never hurts to ask. For example, retirees can sometimes qualify for discounts because they spend more time at home and can simply monitor their property more carefully.

11. If you are in the market for a new home, take its insurance premiums into consideration before buying. A home that is next to a fire hydrant might have a lower insurance premium. If a home is in an earthquake-prone zone, wooden frames have lower premiums because they are more flexible. If a home is in a windstorm-prone area, a brick house will have lower rates than a wood-framed home.

What insurance companies can I trust?

Unfortunately, property insurance companies are in the business of making money and not paying claims. In that regard, I have found that 85-percent of property insurance claims are underpaid by at least $10,000.

Over the past 12 years, my law firm has learned that the best way to prevent our clients from being victimized by greedy insurance companies is *not to buy insurance from them.* Therefore, I suggest purchasing insurance from the following carriers:

- Allied Trust
- Universal North America
- Centauri
- American National Lloyds

If you would like to check out an insurance company beforehand, you can certainly find various rankings online. However, make sure that such rankings aren't sponsored by the very insurance company they are recommending! You can see how well an insurer treats its clients from a complaint index; many state insurance agencies post complaint indexes on their website, and this analyzes how many complaints the state insurance agency receives about a company. The Texas Department of Insurance's complaint indexes can be found at https://www.tdi.texas.gov/consumer/cpportal.html. Other sites, such as Standard and Poor's, A.M. Best, and Moody's, can verify an insurance company's financial health.

Conclusion

We hope this chapter has been helpful in understanding how to look for an insurance policy, how to make sure the policy provides adequate coverage, what to expect from mortgage lenders, and how to get the most bang for your buck. Moving forward, we'll expand on this chapter's information by discussing what is – and is not – covered by a homeowners insurance policy.

CHAPTER THREE

WHAT LOSSES ARE COVERED BY MY POLICY?

In this chapter, we will look at the perils that are covered by insurance – and those that are not. I touched on the concept of perils back in Chapter One. You remember Nathan and Opie, the neighbors with the "Named Perils" and "Open Perils" insurance policies. Well, as promised, we are going to delve more deeply now into what the perils are, whether your policy will cover you for them, and what to do about the things that are not covered.

To refresh your memory, a "**peril**" means an event that could damage your home or your possessions. Not every policy covers every peril, and as always, if you have a current homeowners insurance policy, you must refer to it to learn what perils are covered.

A "**loss**" is the damage that your property suffers as the result of a peril.

An "**exclusion**" in your policy means a loss that is not covered. Some exclusions are for damaging events, like earthquakes and floods, and we will go over the complete list of such events in this chapter. These events are simply excluded from all policies unless you buy special insurance at an additional premium. Other exclusions are more complex – under special circumstances, certain perils won't be covered, even if those perils ordinarily *are* covered. A simple example is fire. Fire is a covered peril – unless you commit arson. If a fire is proved to have been caused by arson, it is excluded from coverage by insurance. An exclusion can also be for a certain item damaged by a peril. For example, if your property is damaged by the weight of a heavy snowstorm, damage to your house is covered, but damage to your fence is excluded.

The definitions and meanings of exclusions are often the subject of lawsuits, particularly when unusual circumstances arise. It is always a good idea to check with an insurance attorney if you think your insurance company is manipulating the definitions of perils and exclusions to avoid paying a valid claim.

Peril vs. Hazard

Sometimes, there is confusion in homeowners insurance discussions over the terms "peril" versus "hazard". This is compounded by the fact that the portion of a homeowners policy that covers *just the structure itself* is sometimes called "hazard insurance." A hazard insurance policy is not a replacement for a homeowners insurance policy because it covers the structure only (roof, walls, flooring, built-in appliances, and attached garages), and will not cover personal property, liability, or living expenses.

A peril is the cause of a loss, a "hazard" is something that increases the chances that a peril will happen and increases the likelihood of a loss. For example, if you have oily rags lying in your garage, and they catch on fire and burn your house down, the oily rags are the hazard, and the fire is the peril.

What are the 16 Named Perils?

There are 16 named perils recognized by most homeowners insurance policies:

1. **Fire and Lightning**. Fire has been defined over the years (and through many court cases) to mean that there is combustion sufficient to generate "flame, glow, or incandescence." Basically, that means a fire must produce light, and that smoke, charring or scorching alone are insufficient to qualify as fire.
    a. Additionally, fires are defined as either "friendly" or "unfriendly."
        i. Unfriendly fires are sometimes also called "hostile" fires. Unfriendly or hostile fire escapes its intended confines.
        ii. Friendly fire is intentional and stays confined, burning where it is supposed to, such as in the fireplace or on the stovetop.
    b. Only unfriendly fires are covered by insurance.
    c. Direct losses by fire include also damages resulting from smoke from an unfriendly fire, or firefighters' attempts to extinguish an unfriendly fire.
2. **Windstorm or hail.** When making a claim for the peril of windstorms or hail, your house's exterior must be damaged before any interior damages can be claimed. What does this mean?

a. Damages caused to your home interior or possessions by dust, rain, sand, sleet, or snow are excluded *unless* the exterior walls/roof are first damaged by the direct action of the windstorm or hail.

   i. You cannot claim damages to your home's contents if you simply left a window open, and a violent windstorm blew buckets of rain into your home.

   ii. If that same window was shattered by that windstorm, however, and buckets of rain blew inside, the contents would be covered.

b. Watercraft, their trailers, and equipment are excluded from this peril's coverage unless they are inside a fully enclosed building.

3. **Explosion**. Damages are covered whether the explosion originates inside your home or outside. There are no exclusions.

4. **Riots or Civil Commotion**. This covers damages caused by civil commotion, and by people who are engaged in civil commotion. Even pillaging and looting are covered if they occur during, and at the location, of the riot. Riots are distinguished from insurrections (which are excluded because they are Acts of War) with this difference: insurrections have the intent to overthrow a duly constituted authority.

5. **Falling Objects.** Obviously, the term "Falling Objects" includes part, or all, of a tree – or perhaps a telephone pole, and aircraft or aircraft parts. But believe it or not, this definition also includes satellites, asteroids, meteors, and space debris!

a. The contents of your house aren't covered under this peril *unless* the outside of your house is damaged first.

b. Another interesting twist – the falling object itself is not covered. So, insurance won't pay for the tree, or an item of yours that falls off the wall and breaks.

6. **Weight of Ice, Snow, or Sleet.** This coverage is restricted to damages actually caused by the weight of these things. So, melted ice that leaks into your home is not covered. There are also restrictions about what structures are covered for such damage; the house itself is covered, but things like patios, fences, and foundations are not.

7. **Accidental Discharge or Overflow of Water or Steam.** Unexpected water damage caused by "discharge, leakage, or overflow" of water from appliances, plumbing, heating, automatic sprinkler systems or air conditioning systems is covered. Tearing out the damaged structure and replacement of the damaged structure is covered, but replacement of the appliance or system is not.

8. **Sudden and Accidental Tearing Apart, Cracking, Burning, or Bulging of Heating or Air Conditioning Systems or of Household Appliances.** The "sudden and accidental" is the key to coverage of this peril. Damage that occurs over time or that was intentionally caused is not covered.

9. **Freezing of Plumbing, Heating, and Other Systems.** The damage to the structure, as well as any appliance lost as a result of that freezing, is covered. The insurance company does expect you to use reasonable means to prevent these damages from happening, such

as maintaining sufficient heat in the building. Thus, you cannot intentionally leave your house unheated in sub-zero temperatures and expect the insurance company to pay if damages occur.

10. **Damage from Car or Vehicle.** In the unusual event that a vehicle crashes into your house, the damage is covered.

11. **Damage from Aircraft.** In the even more unusual event that an airplane crashes into your house, the damage is covered. This is separate from the "falling objects" peril, which covers parts of aircraft that might fall from them as they pass overhead.

12. **Smoke**. Smoke damage is covered, whether it comes from a fire within your house or a fire outside of your house (such as a forest fire, or a fire on a nearby property).

13. **Vandalism/ Malicious Mischief.** This includes damage done to the home in the process of a burglary.

14. **Theft**. This peril is covered if an intruder breaks into your home through a locked door or window. However, most policies have limits on payments. Extra insurance should be purchased for particularly valuable possessions. I will discuss personal property in more depth in Chapter Four.

15. **Sudden and Accidental Damage from Artificially Generated Electrical Current**. This means that sudden, accidental injury to wiring and appliances due to artificially generated currents is covered. Circuitry, electronic components, transistors, and tubes are excluded

from coverage. Artificially generated electrical current is different from lightning (which is natural electricity).

16. **Volcanic Eruption.** This is usually limited to "above-ground" effects of volcanic eruption, such as those damages caused by lava, ash, or other debris. Damage caused by seismic activity (quakes or tremors) that occurs because of a volcanic eruption is usually not covered, as these fall under the earth movement exclusion.

What are Exclusions?

Exclusions can be confusing, and at times they are downright convoluted and seem unfair. It is wise to learn if your home happens to be in an area prone to certain excluded perils (such as floods and earthquakes) so you can purchase additional coverage when needed. Unless you buy special endorsements (extra insurance) that specifically covers these situations, homeowners insurance will not normally cover damages or losses caused by the following things:

1. **Ordinance or Law.** Policies don't cover "damages caused by any ordinance or law enforcement that regulates building construction, repair, or demolition." This is a bit heavy on the legalese, but it actually has to do with keeping your home in compliance with local codes and laws when it comes time to make repairs or do a complete replacement. You see, many communities have laws that state if a building sustains a certain percentage of damage (such as 50 percent), that structure cannot simply be repaired, but instead must be demolished and replaced. When something like that happens, insurance will not cover losses on:

   a. Demolishing the undamaged part of the building.

b. The value of the undamaged part of the building.

c. The increased cost involved in rebuilding the whole structure according to code.

However, a standard homeowners insurance policy does cover a very limited percentage of ordinances; this is usually 10 percent.

2. **Earth Movement**. This includes earthquakes (plus shock waves or tremors that occur before, during, or after volcanic eruption), landslides, mine subsidence, mudflows, and sinkholes or other earth movements like rising or shifting. Direct losses by fire, explosion, or theft that occur as a *result* of earth movement are covered.

3. **Water**. This exclusion can be confusing. It eliminates coverage for certain types of "enumerated water" damage. This includes flooding in all forms: water (and waterborne materials) that have backed up through sewers, sumps or drains, and water (and waterborne materials) that lie below ground and seep through walls, floors, and other structural components. Since a bevy of insurance lawsuits occurred after Hurricane Katrina caused massive damages to hundreds of thousands of homes, the water exclusion has been revised to eliminate:

   a. coverage for water pushed toward shore by wind force

   b. coverage for discharge overflow from containment systems, such as levees or dams

4. **Power Failure**. This is another somewhat confusing exclusion. Whereas many policies do cover damage caused by lightning strikes (power surges), this is not

the same as an interruption of power. The interruption of power to your dwelling is generally not covered if that interruption results from a failure outside of your property. Damages that result from the interruption of power (most usually food spoilage) may be covered under endorsements.

5. **Neglect.** Neglect means that you, as the property's owner, have not used reasonable means to save your property from further damages *at or after a loss*. You cannot collect for damages that you have had a reasonable chance to prevent. Let's say, for example, that a large window was broken in your home due to a falling tree. If you neglect to cover the open window and your furniture and flooring in that room is ruined by a subsequent rainstorm, then the insurance company may refuse your claim for those damages because you did not perform the reasonable means to protect your possessions.

6. **Acts of War**. Acts of War include invasions, insurrections, revolutions, and military coups. Since the events of September 11th, 2001, terrorism has been included as a separate endorsement for protection, but this usually applies only to commercial insurance policies, rather than homeowners insurance policies.

7. **Nuclear Hazard.** This exclusion pertains to nuclear reactions, radiation, and radioactive contamination. Direct loss by fire resulting from a nuclear hazard is covered, however.

8. **Intentional Loss.** Obviously, you cannot file a claim for damages you intentionally caused to your own home, or those that you directed someone else to cause. Arson is a prime example of an "intentional act." This applies even

to other insured persons in the home – just because your wife or husband didn't know you planned to burn the place down doesn't mean they can collect.

9. **Government Action.** This exclusion means that your insurance will not cover losses caused by destruction, seizure, or confiscation of your property if it occurs by order of any government authority. Insurance, for example, will not pay for damages sustained when the police raid your illegal underground gambling ring or drug laboratory. Acts of destruction performed by firefighters to prevent the spread of fire are covered, however.

10. **Concurrent Causation Exclusions.** These exclusions were added to policies in response to "concurrent causation" lawsuits, which resulted in a series of court decisions saying that when a loss results from two causes, one that is excluded and the other which is not, the loss should be covered by the insurance company. Insurance companies were quick to draft in these new exclusions to protect themselves. There are three categories of this type of exclusion:

    a. **Loss caused by weather conditions that contribute to an otherwise excluded peril.** If storm damage (for which you are ordinarily covered) results in a landslide that damages your home (an excluded peril), you are not covered.

    b. **Loss caused by acts or decisions, including failing to do so, of any person, group, organization, or governmental body.** For example, if your local government has failed to enforce building and zoning codes, damages resulting from this failure are excluded.

c. **Loss caused by faulty, inadequate, or defective activities such as planning, design, maintenance, or faulty materials.** Earthquakes are excluded, but suppose your home is damaged because your contractor failed to adequately build your home to be earthquake-resistant, even though the structure is in an earthquake-prone area? This exclusion states that the insurance company still does not have to pay for the damages.

11. **Vacant property exclusions.** A property that has been vacant for more than 60 days may gain new exclusions for losses that otherwise would have been covered. A vacant home might not be covered for damages caused by freezing, pressure of water or ice, theft, or vandalism.

12. **Inevitable losses.** If losses occur over time, and it is difficult to determine when they began, they might become exclusions. These include losses due to:

    a. **Mold, fungus, or wet rot**. This is a controversial area that has resulted in nationwide interest and litigation, and endorsements can be purchased for this type of damage.

    b. **Wear and tear, marring, and deterioration.**

    c. **Mechanical breakdown**, latent defect, inherent vice, or a quality in a property that causes it to damage or destroy itself.

    d. **Corrosion,** such as by smog or rust.

    e. **Smoke** that is caused by industrial or agricultural operations.

f. **Discharge, release, or dispersal of contaminants or pollutants** unless it is caused by one of the named perils for which the property is insured.

g. **Settling, cracking, shrinking, bulging, or expansion** of pavements, patios, foundations, walls, floors, or ceilings.

h. **Birds, rodents, or insects.**

i. **Nesting or infestation,** or secretions that result from a nesting or infestation.

j. **Animals owned by the insured.**

Why do insurance companies refuse to cover some catastrophic events?

We have seen that Acts of War, Earthquakes, and Floods are not covered by standard insurance. Initially, this feels counterintuitive. You might think that of all the things that could happen, insurance should be willing to cover these particularly devastating scenarios. After all, what causes more damage than a massive flood or an earthquake that shakes a city to the ground?

There are a couple of reasons why they do not:

First, insurance companies cannot compute how to charge premiums for the massive destruction that can be caused by such events.

Second, payouts for such damages could be so high that it would drive a company into bankruptcy. Insurance companies are not required to put their businesses at that type of risk.

Remember, too, that special riders can be purchased to include these protections, but they will you cost extra premiums. Still, if your home is in an area that shakes, rattles, rolls...or floods...paying for the extra insurance is probably a solid idea.

Other Insurance Considerations

These are a few miscellaneous terms often associated with homeowners insurance or the purchase of a home:

Collapse Additional Coverage

Until 1984, collapse – the abrupt falling down or caving in of a building or part of the building with the results that it cannot be occupied – was listed as a peril. This was changed because it is illogical to call "collapse" a peril when it is usually caused by another peril and would therefore be a loss. Collapse Additional Coverage is part of all homeowner's policies except H-08, and it covers losses for both the structure and the items inside the structure that were damaged by the collapse. This coverage applies if the collapse is caused by the following:

1. The perils you are insured against (Coverage C).
2. Unknown/hidden decay – if you were aware of the decay and did nothing to remedy it, you cannot claim the loss.
3. Unknown damage caused by insects/vermin – as in No. 2, if you were aware that this damage was occurring and did not remedy the situation, you cannot claim the loss.
4. Weight of the contents (including people and animals).

5. Weight of rain on a roof.
6. Defects in construction materials/methods if the collapse occurs during the construction.

Home warranties

A home warranty includes mechanical failure of individual home parts, including electrical and plumbing systems. A warranty does not protect the house's construction, may or may not cover equipment, expires at a particular time point (e.g., one year), and has exclusions and restrictions you can check. Home warranties cannot be governed by your state department of insurance.

Inflation Guard Endorsement

It is possible to have this option on an insurance policy. Every quarter, such an endorsement will increase the amount of insurance by a percentage of the original value; you determine by what percentage your coverage should increase, from two percent to as much as eight percent. The point of this increase is to ensure that the policy limits rise with inflation and with concurrent increases in construction costs.

Nonbuilding Replacement Cost

Homeowners insurance covers the buildings on your property, but what about structures that aren't buildings? This list includes things like light poles, mailboxes, satellite dishes, or swimming pools. Some of these items, if they are made of fiberglass, metal, plastic, or reinforced masonry, can be covered at replacement cost with a "Replacement Cost Settlement for Certain Non-Building Structures." Structures made out of wood are not covered.

Private Mortgage Insurance

You might hear about other insurance forms, mainly when you buy a home. Usually, lenders need private mortgage insurance (PMI) if the down payment is less than 20-percent of the home's purchase price. PMI covers the lender if the mortgage defaults. Your monthly mortgage payment also requires the PMI premium.

Title Insurance

Title insurance covers you and the lender from monetary liability due to title errors. Though it is unusual, sometimes a property that has had multiple owners will have a bit of hidden history attached to it, and even a diligent search by the title company or your real estate attorney might not turn up everything. A dramatic example of this would be discovering that your beautifully restored historic home was actually bequeathed to the previous owner's nephew 40 years ago, but the Will was lost… until last week. Now, that nephew wants his house, because the person who sold it to you had no right to do so.

Title insurance provides some protection against such situations by providing careful examination of a title's validity, and then indemnification against losses arising out of any undiscovered defects in the title.

When buying a home, you usually pay title insurance as a one-time charge.

Here is an interesting sidenote about title insurance – unlike most other insurance types, title insurance insures against events that occurred in the past (but are as yet unknown or undiscovered), rather than events that will happen in the future.

Final Thoughts on Perils/Exclusions (What Is, and Is Not, Covered)

In this chapter, we outlined homeowners insurance's 16 named perils, and the exclusions to those perils. Not all policies cover all perils, and it is important to know your policy's parameters to determine whether you are safely and fully insured.

The examples and descriptions presented in this chapter were to help you understand these concepts. However, if you should have questions about making a claim or whether a loss is covered, it is always best to consult an expert. Insurance policies are written in legalese that can be quite hard to understand even for experts – this is why insurance cases end up in court. The definitions of perils and exclusions are sometimes easily manipulated. In Chapter Five, we will discuss how to file a claim for losses, and at that time, we'll go into greater detail about when it's time to consult an insurance attorney or advisor.

CHAPTER FOUR

COVERAGE FOR MY PERSONAL PROPERTY

Your personal property is generally covered by a "blanket" policy, meaning that all your personal property is covered by the same insurance amount, rather than having to individually list and insure your possessions. However, if you own particularly expensive items or items that come with a particular risk (such as firearms), these may be excluded from that blanket policy and require separate insurance. A separate, special insurance policy may also include coverage for more perils, as well.

Excluded Personal Property

Here is a list of things that are excluded under blanket coverage:

1. **Anything that you have separately insured**. This is done to avoid coverage duplications. If you have purchased scheduled insurance endorsements for your jewelry, for example, then your jewelry would no longer be protected under your blanket coverage.

2. **Animals, birds, or fish.**

3. **Motor vehicles, their parts, and their equipment**. However, this pertains only to motor vehicles that are required to be registered for use on public roads. Vehicles that are used only to service a residence are covered, such as a riding lawnmower or a tractor. Vehicles that service the disabled are also covered. Golf carts must be covered by separate endorsements.

4. **Aircraft/aircraft parts**. This applies only to the full-size, real thing; model and hobby aircraft are covered.

5. **Hovercraft/hovercraft parts.**

6. **Property belonging to tenants, boarders, or roomers unrelated to the insured (you).** This is a somewhat perplexing exception, so be careful here.

   a. If you are regularly renting out a bedroom, and you own the furniture in that room, the furniture is covered. The renter's property is not covered, so if your renter brings a television set, that television set is not covered since it is the renter's, not yours.

   b. However, if you rent out an "apartment" which has its own cooking and bathing facilities, *even if you own the furniture*, you must seek additional coverage for "Landlord's Furnishings," which provides $2,500 in coverage for appliances and carpeting in apartments on your residence premises.

   c. The moral of the story remains the same: *check your policy*. If you are renting out space, make certain that you understand what is protected by your policy and what might need supplemental insurance.

7. **Personal Property that you have rented out to someone else**. If your cousin is renting your riding lawnmower for the month, it is not covered under your policy. When you rent property to someone else, this is considered a business exposure, and it lies beyond the scope of your homeowners insurance policy.

8. **Business data**. Whether it is physical, like books or papers, or electronically stored (on a drive or computer), business data is not covered. Mostly this pertains to retrieval/replacement costs.

9. **Electronic funds cards**. This includes credit/debit cards, or any cards used for funds deposit, withdrawal, or transfer.

10. **Water/steam.** Water and steam delivered via means of public water supplies are utilities, and not owned by you, the insured. Don't confuse this with the "peril" of water damage. This refers literally to the water itself – so if your pipes burst and you lose $200 worth of water, you cannot be reimbursed for it, even though your water company may still try to bill you for it!

Personal Properties with Limited Coverage

Other types of personal property, while not excluded, can have limited coverage. Depending on your situation and what you own, and especially if the value of your property exceeds these limits, you might wish to seek additional coverage or endorsements. We present here a list of the items that are commonly limited by coverage. Note that in (f), (g), and (h), coverage is also limited to losses from theft only – so if you lose expensive jewelry or silver in a fire, the average insurance policy will not cover the full extent of your loss.

a. **Money, currency, coin collections, scrip, stored value cards (such as prepaid cards), and smart cards**. These are limited to $200, and you may increase coverage to $500 for an additional premium.

b. **Boats, their equipment and motors, and trailers**. The limit here is $1,500. Obviously, if you have a boat worth more than that, it should be separately insured.

c. **Other trailers or semi-trailers**. Again, the limit is $1,500.

d. **Securities, manuscripts, personal records, passports, tickets, stamps**. The limit is $1,500.

e. **Property used primarily for business purposes**. The limit is $2,500.

f. **Property away from the premises used for business purposes**. The limit is $1,500.

g. **Jewelry, watches, precious, and semi-precious stones, furs**. The limit is $1,500 and to loss by *theft only*.

h. **Silverware, silver-plated ware, goldware, gold-plated ware, platinum, pewterware**. The limit is $2,500 and to loss by *theft only*.

i. **Firearms and their equipment.** Limited to $2,500 and to loss by *theft only*.

j. **Portable electronic equipment (that is, equipment which is able to be powered from multiple sources including a car).** Limited to $1,500.

k. **Antennas, tapes, wires, records, disks, other media – while in/upon a motor vehicle.** For example, a CD collection you keep in your car. These are limited to $250.

Scheduled Personal Property Endorsements

If you have valuables that exceed the limits of standard insurance, this is where you turn. You may separately insure items such as antiques, bicycles, jewelry, fine art, firearms, furs, electronics, silverware, goldware, golf equipment, rugs and tapestries, musical instruments, cameras, stamps, cards, or coin collections.

You are not limited to these things, however – if you have any item that is worth more than your blanket policy's limits allow, you may itemize it to be insured to its full value.

For many valuable items, it is a good idea to have periodic appraisals so that you can be certain your possession is fully covered. If you insured your paintings for $35,000 in 2008, better check on them! They could be worth twice as much now, or half as much – and either way, an adjustment is prudent.

So, if you own even one particularly valuable item, you may contact your insurance company about scheduled personal property coverage. Typically, you will be sent a form to complete, on which you indicate the item(s) you want to insure, and how much it is worth. Your insurer will likely want to see an appraisal for the item, to know that it is actually worth as much as you claim.

Scheduled Personal Property Endorsements can offer certain protections that your blanket property insurance doesn't, such as coverage for theft or damage that occurs anywhere in the world (rather than just on your property) and types of loss like misplacement, accidental damage, or "mysterious disappearance." Usually, claims on these endorsements do not have deductibles, either.

The cost of Scheduled Personal Property Coverage is approximately one percent of your insured value, or about $100 for every $10,000 worth of insurance you buy.

Your Personal Property Inventory

It's time for a tough question. Do you have a detailed, accurate, and current inventory of your personal property?

Don't feel too embarrassed if the answer is "no." Most people don't. Or they start a list with good intentions but forget to add to it as time goes by, and they make new property acquisitions.

Now, that being said, you need one. In the event of a loss, your personal property inventory serves two purposes: it helps the insurance company more accurately give you what your property was worth, *and* it helps you remember everything you had! Trying to make a list *after* a loss is difficult, maybe even impossible.

The good news is, making a good personal property inventory isn't hard, especially with modern technology at your fingertips. A video or photographs of the items you own (including their serial numbers and copies of their receipts, if possible) can serve as a great starting point. Then it only takes a bit of extra documentation to make it complete.

Here are the steps to making a personal property inventory. You may use whatever tools you prefer to do this, as long as you get the information into a format that you can access and update when needed. There are even apps available now that will help you inventory your property room by room.

1. List your personal property. You may want to divide the list by rooms or by categories.
2. Don't forget to include property that you keep off-site. Do you have items in storage?
3. Estimate what it would cost to replace each of these things. Keep depreciation/appreciation in mind. Most everyday things depreciate, so be realistic.
4. Keep your sales receipts (or pictures of them) with the list.
5. Keep records of any serial numbers.
6. Keep everything in a safe, fireproof place; if your record is electronic and stored on your computer, keep a backup copy in that safe place, too. A bank's lockbox is an option, as long as this doesn't keep you from updating the list when you buy something new or get a new appraisal.

If this job seems insurmountable, go easy on yourself – it doesn't have to all be done in one day. Keep working on it as time permits or commit to inventorying one room a week until you're finished. Part of an inventory is better than no inventory at all, so try at least to get your more valuable items recorded on your list.

Other Personal Property Considerations and Endorsements

Assisted Living Care Coverage

This endorsement extends coverage for the personal property *and* the potential liability of relatives of yours that are in an assisted care living facility outside of your home.

Business Use

Although homeowners insurance is not intended to cover any of your home's business uses, some policies can cover some business uses like computers and laptops at least partially. However, there are some stipulations:

Computers

Computers present a somewhat complicated insurance scenario. They are *not* excluded from your blanket personal property insurance, meaning that yes, if your computer is stolen or damaged in a fire, you'll probably get covered for the cost of the machine itself. The problem is that in a significant number of cases, damage caused to computers is a result of the peril of Artificially Generated Electrical Current, and that peril's exclusions include tubes, transistors, electronic components, and electronic circuitry – or in other words, most everything your computer is made of. Whoops! The "Special Computer Coverage Endorsement" is therefore a smart idea – it provides open-peril coverage on your computer equipment.

Data Recovery

Generally, most homeowners insurance policies do not pay for data recovery unless a separate endorsement is purchased. This is something of a gray area, though – again, the nature of the damage to computers has a lot to do with whether coverage comes into play or not, and the nature of the data that is lost may also be an issue. Financial data is sometimes recoverable, and intellectual property like pictures may also be.

Daycare Coverage

Many homeowners insurance plans have minimal coverage if you care for a friend's children and are not paid. But if you're paid for daycare at home, you need to buy more insurance to cover your associated liability.

Golf Carts

If you own a golf cart, it is not covered under your standard homeowners insurance policy. The endorsement that will provide coverage is called the "Owned Motorized Golf Cart – Physical Loss Coverage Endorsement." The coverage is for the cart and any accessories or equipment that you have installed on it permanently. You can also elect to include "collision" insurance on this. In some large retirement communities built around numerous golf courses, golf carts are so expensive, so elaborately designed, and so frequently driven, not only on golf courses but throughout the entire community, that entire law practices have sprung up around "golf cart" accidents and lawsuits.

Grave Markers

This may come as a surprise. Mausoleums and other grave markers that you own, even if they are not on your premises, are covered up to $5,000 for losses that are caused by perils insured under Coverage C. This is not an endorsement, but a revision added in 2000.

Other Members of Your Household

This is a relatively new endorsement that was prompted by the increase of "nontraditional" family living situations. In a standard homeowner's policy, a resident of your household who is over 21 and not a relative to you would not be insured. However, the "Other Members of Your Household" provision allows a modification of definition of insured people in your household – it can mean a person of any age or gender who lives with you (the named insured), in a personal relationship or in an expense-sharing relationship.

Tenant's Improvements and Betterments

Back in Chapter One, we discussed the various types of homeowners insurance policies. You may recall that H-04 was the form for renters insurance. It contains all the same insurance as the H-03 policy when it comes to liability and personal property but does not cover the structure itself, which is the landlord's responsibility.

However, as a tenant, you may be allowed to make improvements or installations to your rented dwelling. If you do so, you may insure these improvements for their "use value" to you. This is a bit tricky – you see, any improvements you make to the property become a part of the property and technically belong to the landlord. After all, you cannot take them with you when you leave. However, you can enjoy their use while you still live there.

It is up to the landlord to maintain insurance on the property's value. You may, however, insure your *interest* in the improvements. If they are damaged, you too suffer the loss.

Note, this situation is far more typical of a commercial insurance policy. Businesses frequently must make improvements and changes to properties they rent. However, if you do happen to make significant improvements to a rented dwelling (with the landlord's permission, of course), it may be to your benefit to investigate the Tenant's Improvements and Betterments insurance endorsement.

Conclusion

This chapter has covered Personal Property insurance and its limits, plus how to obtain scheduled insurance on your valuable items. We discussed tips for creating a personal inventory of your possessions. Finally, we covered some of the more common endorsements that can be added to the personal property insurance section of your insurance policy. Definitions and examples were presented simply for ease of understanding. As I always remind you, the best way to assess your homeowners insurance coverage is to read your individual policy and consult an expert with any questions you may have.

CHAPTER FIVE

HOW TO FILE A CLAIM

I have been talking for four chapters about what homeowners insurance is, why you need it, how much it costs, and what it covers. Now, we have arrived at the point where all of this knowledge pays off.

Your home has been damaged. Here is what you should do:

Getting Started

Your insurance policy contract requires you to let the insurance company know as soon as possible if you have a property damage claim. Failure to do so within the period specified in your contract could result in denial of your claim. It is vital to keep in mind that even if you have to abandon your home, you must inform your insurance carrier as quickly as possible.

Talk about pressure! It sounds as though, if you don't grab the phone the minute the storm is over, your insurance company will not only refuse to help you, but they might even turn you into their office joke this month. Memes of you will soon be cropping up all over the Internet. You'll be the opening monologue joke on *The Tonight Show.*

Take a deep breath. Going through the process of filing a claim is no one's idea of a picnic, but we're going to get you through it smoothly. After the event is over, take stock of your situation, get a grip on what you're dealing with, prepare yourself mentally, and then contact the insurance company.

Here are some pointers on how to take the pain out of the process. These tips will help before, during, and after you have made contact:

1. **NOTE WHO YOU TALK TO AND WHAT THEY TELL YOU.** When you make a call, be sure to have some way to take notes. Take down the name of the person you speak with, the date and time, as well as any phone, case, or claim numbers they give you. The same goes for anyone who comes to your home to inspect the damage – whether it is a contractor, insurance adjuster, or police officer.
2. **KEEP ALL YOUR RECORDS TOGETHER.** Have a folder, box, basket, or any other sort of container for all your paperwork concerning this claim. The most important thing is keeping information where you can find it quickly – and beyond that, you can be as neat and organized as you wish, employing labels and sticky notes or whatever suits you. You can even scan it or type it all into your computer if you can remember to do so for every piece of information. The frustration this will prevent is worth the effort.
3. **CONTACT THE AUTHORITIES FIRST, IF NECESSARY.** In particular cases, before filing a claim, your insurance company will need an official report from law enforcement. Contact the authorities if:

a. Criminal activity is involved.

b. Someone is injured on your property.

c. There has been a fire on your property.

Be certain to give all the relevant information to the officer and keep copies of your report. In some cases, modern police departments allow online filing of criminal incidents, and an officer will follow up with you as needed.

4. **REVIEW YOUR POLICY, IF POSSIBLE**. If it has been a while since you bought or reviewed your policy, look over your policy before calling. Make note of any questions you have or anything you don't understand prior to the call. This will help avoid surprises and better prepare you for the conversation with the representative.

5. **TAKE PICTURES OF THE DAMAGE**. It is better to take too many pictures than not have enough. Exercise your inner Spielberg and photograph the damage from multiple angles and in good light. Get pictures of things that relate to the damage as well, such as resulting indoor damages and the measures you have taken to prevent further damage from occurring.

6. **MAKE URGENTLY NEEDED REPAIRS**. You will recall that an insurance company often will not pay for damage caused to your possessions as a result of damaged property. So, for example, if you have broken windows, holes in the roof or walls, or anything else that will allow wind, water, or other damaging elements to further damage your property or possessions, get them covered up as soon as you can. You are contractually responsible to mitigate extra damages during a calamity,

and this includes preventing third parties from on-site injuries.

a. **BUT DON'T ENDANGER YOURSELF**. Nobody expects you to climb on a dangerously damaged, ice-covered roof. Do what you can safely and get professional help to do the rest. Save any receipts for reimbursement.

b. **TAKE PICTURES OF YOUR TEMPORARY REPAIRS**. This is to show the insurance company that you did what was expected to protect your property.

Contacting the Insurance Company

The sooner you call, the sooner you're going to recover.

Insurance companies now offer the ability to file online. This is fine for small, clear issues – such as a single broken window or smoke damage from a grease fire in the kitchen. However, if your claim is complicated (i.e., your house has become uninhabitable) and/or the damage is seriously expensive (i.e., your roofing and siding were both destroyed by hail damage), it is best to speak directly with a representative from your insurance company.

Your first talk with the insurance company may be stressful – remember, you've been through an ordeal – but go easy on yourself. The most important thing to do in this first call is to timely convey that damage has occurred and to get yourself in line for an appraiser to come survey the damage as soon as possible. There can be quite a waitlist for appraisers if a storm has done damage to a widespread amount of properties, for example. At any rate, the sooner the process is started, the sooner your life can get back to normal.

You do not have to have every piece of information at hand during this first call. There will be time for follow-up calls and/or emails. But do have the following information ready:

- Your Policy Number
- Your address
- The type of claim (winter storm, fire, flood, etc.)
- A description of the damage done to your home and belongings

Remember that just reporting the damage to the representative *does not mean that the claim is filed.* This is only the first step. The claim is a full process that includes initial contact with the insurance company, claim evaluation, discussions, and resolution/settlement. If the claim is approved, the insurance company distributes funds to pay for the contractor, repairs, and/or replacements. I make this distinction because it is possible for you to decide against going ahead with a claim immediately or proceeding at all, for whatever reason.

Document the Process Throughout

Be smart about your claim by documenting the process. At the very least, it will keep you from having to search for things or hunt down copies. But if the claim ends up being in dispute, a good record of events will be important to arguing your side of the case (we'll talk about that in Chapter Seven). Keep a record of everything, through documents (including official reports), photos or videos, appraisals, and the list of everyone you speak to. Remember to do the following:

1. Take notes of what your representative tells you, but also ask them to send you an email confirming what you have discussed and detailing any documents or information they need from you. Don't delete these email exchanges!

2. Take close-up photographs of all the debris, hailstones you found, damage to your house, other buildings, and damage to personal property—before cleaning or throwing away something.

3. Make a list of everything that is part of your claim, including the damage itself, all the items damaged, destroyed, or stolen, and anything else that will be a part of the claim. If you're claiming damage to your personal possessions, make a list of their values. The insurance company will want this information.

4. Save every receipt from expenses you incur as a result of this incident. If you must buy a huge tarp to cover a hole in the roof, or if you must hire a contractor to move the fallen tree from your window, ask for receipts and keep *everything*. Don't forget to:

    a. Keep receipts from expenses incurred through an unlivable home. Your insurance company will compensate you for costs involved in housing your family while your home is being repaired if the home is unlivable. You can review the concept of a home that is unlivable in your policy or discuss it with your agent. Note that if you have free accommodations –

such as with a relative, a friend, or a second home – there is no reimbursement to assert.

b. Keep documents of expenses or losses incurred if your home was also your office and you cannot work there while repairs are underway.

Working with Claims Adjusters to Determine Scope

Adjusters often work directly for your insurance company. Still, insurance companies sometimes hire out their claims to an "independent adjuster," particularly if there has been a large influx of claims, such as when a storm damages many homes in an area. If you want a second opinion and don't mind paying the fee, you may also hire your own adjuster from a third party; this person is known as a "public adjuster."

An adjuster wants to create a clear scope of loss on the initial visit, to assist you in their obligation to prove the loss. This means that you (or your attorney) and the adjuster can walk through your home or company and agree on exactly what was damaged or destroyed as a result of the risk insured against. It is wise to take notes during the visit because a great deal of detail will be discussed. You can ask if you can make an audio or video record of the meeting on your phone, but I recommend that you do not allow the insurance company to record meetings.

The extent of the damage must be specified. The breadth of loss must include descriptions of distinctive features, openings, casements, details, moldings, and other architectural characteristics, as well as materials such as moldings, floors, wall coverings, and fittings.

On the first inspection, the scope of loss must be as complete and accurate as feasible. During an initial assessment, the adjuster should not:

- Take a quick look around and ask the insured to fill out a property loss form at his leisure.
- Leave the insured with blank forms, except for supplemental items discovered after the initial scope was completed.
- Take a partial scope and attempt to complete the rest later.
- Unreasonably rely on another person's expertise.
- Make promises they won't be able to keep.
- Make a payment commitment before agreeing on the amount of loss and claim.
- Commit to coverage when the facts and insurance conditions or exclusions present an issue.

If necessary, an adjuster will inform you if they need to retain experts in the assessment and repair of the type of the property concerned. The repair and replacement work will be bid on by these professionals based on the agreed-upon "scope."

The scope of the work is an assessment and an agreement of how much actually needs to be done. A "scope of work" document usually contains a timeline, milestones, deliverables, reports and a description of the end product that is expected.

The scope of repair/replacement work can vary as new details are discovered, so the adjuster's initial scope is only a preliminary assessment based solely on visual damage. Before preparing any repair estimates, the adjuster must provide you a copy of the agreed-upon scope. The adjuster provides a copy of the scope of loss to two general contractors. Each contractor can prepare detailed estimates of repair costs based on the adjuster's scope of loss, so that the adjuster can find the lowest bidder.

The adjuster should generate a cost estimate for repairs to compare to the contractors' bids utilizing the scope of damage and estimating systems like Xactimate. The adjuster may try to have you sign the paperwork agreeing to the scope of loss once the adjuster and the insured have decided on the scope. You, however, should never sign any document without speaking with an experienced home insurance attorney.

What you should NOT say to the claims adjuster

When you are having a conversation with an adjuster, it is very important to keep the proper frame of mind. This is not like having a conversation with a friend or confidant. The adjuster is listening for reasons to deny your claim. Therefore, treat this the same as you would treat an interview with an officer of the law. Remember that you should not permit your conversation to be recorded by the other party. Then, follow these guidelines:

1. Don't disclose unnecessary personal information, such as your employment status. Your name and contact information are all the adjuster needs to know about you.
2. Don't give out unnecessary details of the accident. The adjuster can know the time, date, location, and what happened (i.e., hail damaged my roof; a fire broke out

in our kitchen), and any possible witness contact information. The adjuster does not need to know what everyone was doing beforehand, what thoughts raced through your mind, or all the things you wish you had done to prevent this incident.

3. Remember you are not an expert. Don't speculate on what caused the loss, elaborate on the surrounding circumstances, or make assumptions about any damage you believe you may have experienced. That is the adjuster's job.

4. Never apologize, or admit to any form of wrongdoing, not even innocent mistakes or miscalculations. Any acknowledgment of fault can jeopardize a claim.

5. Don't refer to your current state of health. This is tricky because almost the first thing anyone asks in a conversation is, "How are you today?" and our automatic response is something like, "Fine, how are you?" Deflect the question and move the conversation along.

6. Answer reasonable questions as simply as possible, and then stop talking. It's human nature to want to "fill in" a silence by adding details or follow-up information, but it is not your job to entertain the adjuster. The more you talk, the more likely it is that you'll say something that might damage your claim. If the adjuster's questions seem unreasonably personal or irrelevant, you don't have to answer them at all, and it's definitely a warning sign that you're dealing with a bad adjuster. See Chapter Seven's section on "How Good is Your Insurance Adjuster?" for more details.

Finally, remember that if you have retained an insurance lawyer, you need not say anything to the claims adjuster or anyone else. Direct all inquiries to your attorney. Problem solved!

How long is this going to take?

That's the million-dollar question, isn't it? And of course, the answer is not simple. Claims for straightforward damage can be quite brief and settled up within a few weeks. Complicated claims will naturally take longer, perhaps months, to resolve. A total loss (like the home needing to be rebuilt) might take as long as two years.

Other factors can come into play, as well. If an ice storm or tornado severely damaged the region, people and businesses making claims just like yours will be numerous. Contractors and appraisers will be harder to find. Or perhaps your home was damaged by two factors at once, such as a storm and a resulting fire, so depending on your insurance coverage, you might have to make separate claims. For example, if you have flood insurance from a specialized company, but wind damage is covered by your homeowners policy, a separate claim will be necessary.

Try not to be discouraged if things don't move as fast as you would like. Have patience and enjoy the victories as they happen. Eventually, things will return to normal.

Now, I tell you that with the following warning: if you believe your insurance company is intentionally dragging its feet, giving you the runaround or an unfair deal, you don't have to simply accept this treatment. In Chapter Seven, I will discuss the ways you can handle a dispute. Disputes will, in fact, increase the amount of time a claim takes, but this may well be preferable to having the insurance company severely undercut your damages.

Avoid These Mistakes When Filing a Claim

Here is a list of a few common mistakes that can slow matters down considerably or make trouble for you later. Try to avoid these to make the process run far more smoothly!

1. Don't be late in filing the claim – but if you are late due to circumstances beyond your control, be prepared to explain (and prove) why.

2. Don't forget to save, and submit, receipts for everything. You won't receive reimbursement for anything you leave out. This is why having an inventory of your damaged property is so important. You can keep track of what the insurance company has, and has not, paid for.

3. Beyond those emergency tactics used to prevent further damage, do not repair anything until the insurance company has approved the repair. All of the agreements regarding necessary repairs and costs should be in writing.

4. Don't start cleaning up and throwing everything away. There is an urge to clean up, yes, but do so only after you have thoroughly documented damages and, if at all possible, the appraiser sees all of the damages as well.

5. Don't assume you must use the insurer's vendors. You have a right to hire your own professionals: contractors, public adjusters, engineers, etc. In most cases, it is in your best interests to do so. I will discuss this more in Chapter Six.

6. Don't assume the insurance company is right. If you have doubts, encounter problems, or have a claim that is extremely complex, there are methods you can use

to make certain you get what you deserve, which we will discuss in Chapter Seven. Remember that the adjuster works for the insurance company and is looking out for the insurance company's best interests. You have the right to hire your own team of experts to assist you with the claims procedure, such as a highly experienced attorney who specializes in insurance claims.

Time Limits on Filing a Claim

Generally, in the United States, claims need to be filed within a year (or two) of the incident, but you should confirm your deadline with your policy/agent. In each state, laws may affect the amount of time you have to file a claim. Contact an attorney early to avoid any issues.

Remember that there are also *multiple* deadlines within a single claim. Be certain you don't let these slip by as you are moving through the process:

1. Deadline to notify of a loss.
2. Deadline to submit documentation.
3. Deadline to dispute the claim/obtain legal help.

When not to File a Claim

Sometimes, the damage done is small enough that you must ask yourself whether filing a claim is worth it. You might consider your deductible as a guideline here. If your deductible is $500 and you need to replace a $450 door, filing a claim is not necessary. Even if that door is $650, you might consider simply paying for the damage out of pocket. Why would you do this?

- Sometimes, reporting a claim may result in the increase of your rates.
- Sometimes, reporting a claim might even cause the cancellation of your policy.

Your claim history follows you for up to seven years. The Comprehensive Loss Underwriting Exchange (CLUE) is a database used by insurers to decide premium rates. Any time you make an insurance claim, a record of it will likely be kept on CLUE. This can be true even if you have only called to inquire about a claim, so all insurance companies will be aware of all the claims you make. The more extensive your claims history is, the worse your record will look.

Many people avoid filing claims out of fear it will dramatically increase their premiums. A single claim does not always increase your premium. Your insurance company might even offer accident forgiveness. However, if you file multiple claims within a certain time period, this can cause your insurance premiums to go up.

If the damages are extensive, however, do not be afraid of filing a claim. That's what insurance is for. A claim is not a "bad" thing – it ensures that repairs are made, maintains (or even increases) the value of your home, and replaces your damaged possessions. Your life can return to normal.

You may talk to your insurance agent about your claim and whether or not it will raise your premiums based on your history, and if so, by how much.

How is a Claim Paid?

Payments are usually made by check or wire transfer.

The complexity of the claim will determine how payments come. Simple matters may result in one payment from the insurance company. More expensive repairs might involve two payments – half to the contractor up front, and half upon completion. Extremely complex claims, like a fire that requires the replacement of the house and its contents, will require that multiple payments be made over time. Separate payments might come for your real property and personal property. And, if you are in dire need (such as, your house is unlivable), an initial payment may come to you very quickly, to reimburse you for immediate expenses such as food and lodging.

In most cases, even if you accept the insurance company's payment for the damages, if you find further damages, you have the option of submitting another claim. The scope of damages is not always immediately apparent. Once more, it is important to photograph, document, and save all of your evidence.

You may not have sole control over the money distributed to repair your residence. If the structure of your home is damaged and you have a mortgage, the insurance company's check will probably be made out to both you *and* your lender. This is simply because the lender still has a significant investment in the quality of your home. Your lender might insist on holding all the funds in escrow, releasing them to the contractor as the work is completed, and they may even require an inspection before releasing the final payment. A comparable situation applies to owners of condominiums or co-ops, as the appearance and value of these units has a direct impact on the surrounding units.

Late Reporting

Making a late claim means you didn't make your claim when everybody else did so (within the first few weeks). Regulations are in place requiring you to report damage as quickly as possible, so if you didn't, you must justify why.

It is extremely important for homeowners to read their insurance contracts thoroughly to understand the expectations and requirements that are placed upon them as the insured. Most insurance policies contain wording that require the insured to provide prompt or immediate written notice to the insurance company or one of its agents in the event of a loss. This time limit can be anywhere from 30 days to a year depending on the insurer. Waiting too long to file a claim could be used by your insurance company as grounds to prove that you are not in compliance with a condition in your homeowners insurance policy, giving them the right to deny your claim for coverage. But why is this a requirement?

To put it simply, homeowners must be able to prove that the damage to their home was the result of a covered event and not caused by some other secondary cause that exceeds the responsibility of the insurance company. If a recent tornado were to have damaged your roof, it is in your best interest to file a claim as soon as possible before the damage has time to escalate into further destruction that can be denied coverage under your policy's negligence clause. If an appraiser finds that the damage to your home could have been prevented by filing a claim more quickly, you may be held financially responsible for the repairs.

Things can become much more complicated if the damage to a person's home is not readily apparent. Let's say, for example, that a violent windstorm rocks your area, causing a tree to snap and fall. While you heard a loud bang and suspect something may have struck your house, when you inspect the area the morning after, you see no damage other than the fallen tree in your backyard. Unbeknownst to you, the tree did indeed hit your house, punching a basketball-sized hole in your roof outside of your view. Eight weeks after the windstorm, a thunderstorm causes several hours of torrential rain to pour through your roof, causing extensive flood damage. Your insurance company proceeds to deny your claim, claiming that your home's damage was caused by your failure to repair your roof.

In any case, it is always best to thoroughly investigate all potential claims as soon as possible after a disaster.

The most common excuses for late reporting are:

- I was out of town.
- I was severely ill.
- I believed the loss was deductible.
- I didn't see the damage.

To begin the process of filing a late claim, you should write a letter explaining why. Here is the format I suggest, and of course, you will need to tailor the letter to fit your specific case.

(DATE)

Attention: (Adjuster or Agent)

XYZ Business Insurance

100 First Street North

Town, State 90000

RE: (YOUR NAME)

Loss date: ________________

Policy#: __________________

Claim#: _________________

Dear _____________________

(Now amend the following paragraphs to apply to your situation.) On __________________(date), I had hail damage to my house.

Because I didn't go to my roof after the storm, I didn't know my house was destroyed. I found a leak in my roof on ________________(date). That made me look at the roof. On ___________________(date), I submitted my loss report to your office.

This is a fair notice of failure under the circumstances. If your company reserves the right to refuse late details, please notify me in writing within ten days of this letter's date.

Truly yours,

(YOUR NAME)

(Your contact information)

What's Next?

The focus of this chapter has been on getting the ball rolling when it comes to filing a claim. We've discussed the importance of documenting the process, what the insurance company will expect from you, what you can expect from them in return, what mistakes to avoid, and what measures you can take if your filing is late.

The next step is actually making the repairs to your home.

CHAPTER SIX

MAKING THE REPAIRS

You and your insurance company have come to an agreement on estimated costs for a repair. Now, it is time to get the work done.

As with every other facet of a homeowners insurance claim, the extent and complication of your needed repairs will determine how much oversight the insurance company insists on having, and how relaxed they are about distributing the money.

Proof of minor damages could mean they send you money to cover the full cost and have little care about who does the work. Or, if payment comes in two parts—half up-front and half upon completion—your insurance company may casually accept a photograph or a letter of confirmation attesting to the completed work. With bigger jobs, they may insist on a detailed accounting from the contractor, as well as an inspection upon the job's completion.

You can prepare yourself for these contingencies by asking questions ahead of time or while your claim is processed. Find out specifically what they require for completion of the claim. If you know your company requires a letter, inspection, or detailed accounting, this will simply become part of the process. You may let your contractor(s) know, so that the need for extensive or detailed reports will not come as a surprise to them, and you can schedule an inspection. These are hurdles, yes, but knowing they are coming makes them much easier to clear.

Outline of the Process

A homeowners insurance claim usually happens in this order:

1. You contact your insurance company to alert them of the damage to your home.

2. A claims adjuster comes to your home, reviews the damage, and then develops an estimate of the costs for repairs.

3. The insurance company sends you a check for the actual cash value of the damaged object(s). Note that if you have replacement cost coverage, they supplement the difference to you when the repairs are completed.

4. You collect bids from one or more contractors, in which they list the costs of materials and labor. You submit these bids to your insurance company for its approval.

5. You select a contractor to repair your home.

6. When the repairs are complete, you or the contractor submit the required proof of completion to your insurance company. As mentioned above, if you have replacement cost coverage, the remainder of the funds are released to you.

Replacement Cost vs. Actual Cash Value

In Chapter One, we discussed the difference between actual cash value, replacement cost, and extended (or guaranteed) replacement cost. Check your policy, but your home's structure is probably covered at replacement cost, whereas your possessions are probably covered at actual cash value.

Let's briefly cover how to calculate the "actual cash value" of your possessions. Here is a simple example:

You might have paid $2,400 for your dining room set, but that was 10 years ago, and now, its "actual cash value" is $1,200. So, that is all that your policy will pay to replace it.

> How does the insurance company determine the actual cash value of an item? Different insurance companies may use different techniques, but here is a fairly common one:

$$R \times (E - C) / E = ACV$$

R = replacement cost of the item
E = expected lifespan of the item
C = current life of the item
ACV = actual cash value

So, if that dining room set has an expected life of 20 years, the actual cash value comes to:

$$\$2{,}400 \text{ x } (20\text{–}10) / 20 = \$1{,}200.$$

Items like electronics depreciate very quickly. Let's do a similar equation looking at the actual cash value of a laptop. We'll use the *Business News Daily*'s estimate that a laptop's useful lifespan is, at most, five years (though it may be as few as three years), and we'll estimate that you spent $600 on your laptop and had it for four years.

R × (E - C) / E = ACV

R = replacement cost of the item
E = expected lifespan of the item
C = current life of the item
ACV = actual cash value

The actual cash value of your damaged laptop comes to:

$600 x (5-4) / 5 = $120.

Therefore, you will only receive $120 with which to buy a new laptop.

Note: if an item is *older* than its useful lifespan, the replacement value is $0.

Getting replacement costs for personal items is tricky, so it is wise to have an extremely detailed inventory of your household items that includes their defining characteristics. Do not list that you own a "sofa" if that sofa included three reclining seats, heat and massage components, electronics chargers, cupholders, and a storage compartment and was upholstered in fine Corinthian leather, and therefore, would cost substantially more to replace. Keeping serial numbers and receipts of your original purchase prices is a smart way to ensure that your compensation is fair. Remember, too, that if you own truly valuable items, it might be in your best interest to insure them separately, as we discussed in Chapter Four.

How do Replacement Cost Payments Work?

If my home is damaged, and I have a replacement cost policy, typically the process goes this way: I file the claim, and the insurance company gives me the actual cash value to begin repair and replacement. When the repair/replacement is complete, I then submit documentation to prove the actual costs of the job. The insurance company reviews the documentation, and then pays the remainder of the replacement cost up to the policy limits. Deductibles are not reimbursable.

If my home is damaged, and I have an actual cash value policy, the process simply ends after the initial payment for repair/replacement. I do not get to submit follow-up documentation or reimbursement for the difference in insurance payment and the full costs of repair/replacement.

ESTIMATE vs. BID

This is an important difference! When the insurance company sends an appraiser to look at the damage, that appraiser will generate an "estimate" of the costs involved in the repairs. Often, an appraiser and/or the insurance company will use software to generate an estimate, based on data like previous repairs done in your area for that type of damage.

A "bid" comes from a contractor: it is a more detailed report, specifying the scope of the work and the amount that the contractor will charge to do the repairs. We will discuss dealing with disputes further in Chapter Seven but take note: if your insurance company has given an estimate and your contracting bids are coming in much higher, they should probably reconsider their estimate.

Tips for Finding Contractors

When it is time to choose a contractor to do the work, there are several steps you can take to make it a more productive experience. Your insurance company may require a certain number of bids so they can determine the cost of the work, but it is always smart to get at least three bids. How do you obtain three or four reliable bids from good contractors?

1. **LISTEN UP!** Listen to word-of-mouth recommendations. If someone you trust has a glowing critique of a company (or a scathing list of complaints), perk up your ears. If you are in an area where damage is widespread, it shouldn't be difficult to get recommendations. Beware of people who recommend relatives, "Oh, my nephew knows how to do that," or worse, themselves, "I can take care of that for $500!". You are looking for licensed, experienced contractors.

2. **CHECK IT OUT**. You may check with national associations, building inspectors, and even supply businesses (like lumber or siding) to see which contractors are trusted to regularly meet code and pay their bills on time. Check the contractor's status with your local Better Business Bureau and the consumer protection agency at work in your state. These entities can tell you if a contractor has a history of problems.

3. **HAVE A CONVERSATION**. Conduct an initial interview with each of your potential contractors over the phone or by email. *Let the contractor know that this is a repair covered by your homeowners insurance policy.* Ask the following questions:

a. Do they handle projects like yours?

b. Can they provide referrals? This includes financial referrals such as their suppliers, and customer referrals.

c. Who are their subcontractors, and how long have they worked together?

d. Would they be doing other projects at the same time as yours? This will let you know how much attention your project will receive, and if you are a priority.

4. **MEET IN PERSON**. When you have three or four good prospects, meet in person. This meeting's purpose is to let them see the damage, give you an estimate (a bid) for their work, and answer your questions. Listen to your gut. If you don't feel comfortable with the answers you get, or something feels "off" about the conversation, these could be warning signs that, at the very least, you and this contractor will not work well together.

5. **GET A BID**. The contractor should be willing to write a bid for you, detailing the scope of the job, what they will charge for the job, and the projected length of time it will take. When getting a bid, make certain that the bid breaks down these cost factors for you to see:

   a. Materials

   b. Labor

   c. Other overhead

   d. Profit margin

As you compare bids, you can pay attention to these categories and note, for example, if one contractor's materials costs seem inexplicably lower or higher than the other contractors' bids.

6. **CHOOSE YOUR CONTRACTOR**. It is tempting to choose the cheapest bid automatically – if your insurance company will spend $10,000 for your new roof, and Cousin Bill's Roofing bids $7,000 for the job, you might see yourself pocketing that extra $3,000. Before you jump onto the "cheapest" bid, however, consider whether the "cheapest" bid is noticeably lower than the others. This contractor may be cutting corners, using cheap materials, failing to understand the real scope of the work, or having other problems prompting them to make desperate grabs for jobs. Be careful. In reality, communication with a contractor is more important than price – it is far better to pay a bit more and have a good relationship with your contractor than to exchange a few hundred dollars for a lack of feedback or information.

Doing the Repairs Yourself

Contractors are expensive and the idea of putting your home into someone else's hands may be scary. You've heard horror stories. Things go wrong. The work takes forever! Someone does an awful job and then disappears with your money! There are liens! There are lawsuits!

After hearing enough of these contractor nightmares from your coworkers, friends, and relatives, it strikes you that the best solution might be to make the repairs yourself. That's a tempting idea, especially if you really do have knowledge or experience with the repairs in question.

There are really two parts to this possible solution to home repairs: *can* I do the repairs myself, and *should* I do the repairs myself? So, one at a time, let's examine the options.

Can I Fix My Own House?

This version assumes that you do indeed have the tools, skills, experience, and physical capability to perform home repairs. We'll take that as a given for the moment. So, the question is, will your insurance company let you do it?

It depends on a number of factors, but it's the insurance company that will tell you "yes" or "no." They look at:

- The severity of the damage.
- The complexity of the repairs – and in the case of technical work like power or plumbing, whether you have a license to do such work.
- The amount of supervision they believe you would need.
- If your jurisdiction requires certain licensing or permits to perform said work.

What's more, if you have a mortgage, your mortgage lender will also get a say in whether or not you are permitted to do your own repairs. Remember, your lender has a strong motivation to maintain your home's value, thus a strong motivation to make certain that your home is repaired correctly and well.

Should I Fix My Own House?

Even if your insurance company says, "Sure! Go ahead, give it a try!", don't jump on that bandwagon yet. If you *don't* have the tools, skills, experience, and physical capability to perform home repairs, then the answer is definitely "no." You should consider a number of factors before committing yourself to a home repair project:

- **Safety first.** This is not the time to learn complex carpentry or electrical wiring, and it's not the time to believe you are half your age. Even relatively simple jobs like replacing a few roof tiles involve hazards like climbing ladders and balancing on your rooftop. Be honest with yourself about your limits, both mental and physical. If you have a bad back and knees, do you want to spend two days tiling a floor? Do you want to paint if the fumes give you headaches?
- **Will you be aware of the full extent of the damage?** If your house has more extensive damage than either you or the appraiser realized, an experienced contractor will be more likely to see it and understand what they are looking at. You can submit their findings to the insurance company to supplement your claim. Would you be as observant or knowledgeable?
- **Will you actually save any money?** You might have to buy a lot of equipment to get the job done. You might have to pay somebody to repair the damage you do, and be warned, your insurance company does not have to pay for fixing your mistakes. If you don't do a respectable job, you could affect the value of your home.
- **Is the money you'll save really worth your time and effort?** Will you have to take off work? Give up four weekends in a row? Lose half your summer?

Here is one final consideration. If you have minor damage and know you can fix it yourself at cost close to your deductible, it's probably not worth filing a claim at all. As we discussed, claims, especially multiple claims, can cause your rates to increase or may even lead to cancellation of your policy.

Yes, I'm Going to Fix My Own House!

If you go through all those considerations and the answer is "Yes," that is, the insurance company says it's all right, and you think that you can handle making the repairs yourself, then here is a breakdown of the steps in the process. This is the list I provided earlier, supplemented to show the differences that occur when you decide to DIY.

1. You contact your insurance company to alert them of the damage to your home.

2. A claims adjuster comes to your home, reviews the damage, and then develops an estimate of the costs for repairs.

3. The insurance company sends you a check for the actual cash value of the damaged object(s). Note that if you have replacement cost coverage, the difference will be supplemented to you at the end of the job.

4. You collect bids from one or more contractors, in which they list the costs of materials and labor. This is a good idea even if you plan to make the repairs yourself. Contractors will provide a professional assessment of the cost and scope of the work, seeing things that you might have missed.

5. If your insurance company gives you permission to do your own repairs, confirm with them that you do plan to make the repairs yourself. It is important to clear-

ly understand how the insurance company determines what and when they will pay you.

6. You want to ensure that you receive fair pay for the work you do. However, toward that end, you must be honest and clear with your insurance company about what you plan to do, and how you plan to do it. Deliberately withholding information from your company is fraudulent behavior.

Remember that this is a flexible situation. You may be able to complete some of the repairs on your own while still using a contractor for more difficult or challenging tasks. Jobs such as painting, replacing doors or simple accessories, or removing debris might easily be in your capabilities. You might even ask your insurance company to count the money you "earn" with your labor against your deductible total. There is no harm in asking questions or working out arrangements that are beneficial to both you and the insurer.

Do I Get to Keep Any Leftover Money?

At the end of the process, when everyone has been paid, any money remaining is probably yours to keep. Your policy might include information on what has to happen to any claim money that is leftover at the end of the job. Most often, though, the homeowner simply gets to keep the remainder. Of course, this can feel like a lucky little bonus, especially after going through a home-repair ordeal. Remember, however, that this is really about restoring your home to its value and enjoyability. Approaching a claim as a way to "make money" is really missing the point of the entire process.

Moreover, this is a matter that requires your complete honesty. If the insurance company asks for an accounting of how the money was spent, you must provide it. You cannot invent charges, pad the bills, or lie to the insurance company about how much things cost, or how much money is left over. To do so is to commit insurance fraud, a crime that can result in fines and even imprisonment, as well as getting your policy cancelled with truly little chance of ever getting another one!

The Easy Claim!

There are tens of thousands of homeowners insurance claims filed each day. Many are handled swiftly, fairly, and with good results. Appraisals and agreements happen, documents and photos provide all the evidence needed, money is on the way, and repairs are precise and perfect. Life can get back to normal. I certainly hope that is the case for you.

But if things go awry, there is no need to suffer alone or deal with the insurance company head-to-head all by yourself. So, let's move on to discuss what to do when a claim doesn't go the way it should!

CHAPTER SEVEN

CLAIM DISPUTES: GETTING WHAT YOU DESERVE

There is damage to your home, and you file a claim against your policy. That's why bought insurance in the first place! You've made timely payments for years. Now, it's the company's turn to help you get your life back in order. If your claim is valid, it is their job – and their duty – to do so.

Sometimes, they will. Other times, it seems they are less interested in repairing your life than they are in keeping your money in their bank account. How do they do this? Most of the time, if they can get you to take $15,000 instead of the $25,000 your claim is really worth, they will do it. And if they can find a way to frame your home's damages in such a way that your policy will not cover it, they will take advantage of that.

This is a hard fact to accept, but when you call in to report a claim, *your insurance company will immediately begin looking for reasons to reject it.* Even the nicest claims manager out there is reporting to a boss who is watching that bottom line. Sure, your insurance company may care about you, but I promise you they care about themselves more.

Despite the upheaval of your life, you have done your part. You have kept the receipts, made the calls, met the deadlines, answered the questions, yet your insurance company is not making a fair offer. Or worse, they're not making any offer at all: they deny your claim for reasons you think are wrong. This can, and does, happen frequently.

You are not powerless. In this chapter, we'll discuss your options for disputing the insurance company's decision.

The Insurance Adjuster's Responsibilities

Once you report a loss, an adjuster is assigned as your primary point of contact with the insurance company. Remember that *the adjuster works for the insurance company.*

The primary responsibilities of an adjuster are to investigate, negotiate, and resolve your claim. They will need to communicate with the insurance company's risk manager and others, evaluate the damage, and assign a value to the loss][;]=. Adjusters can draw on a wealth of experience from similar losses to assist you in making decisions. They also hire consultants like accountants, engineers, architects, and other professionals. A coverage determination is made once they gather enough information. The adjuster will move forward with a settlement if this is positive.

The positions your adjuster takes on coverages and losses may differ from yours. Although the insurer will strongly support the adjuster's decision, the adjustment process is one of negotiation, and your connection with the adjuster, as well as your ability to justify your position with facts, can affect the final settlement.

Start off on the right foot by simply being on your best behavior. An easy and cost-free way to improve the chances that your settlement is prompt, accurate, and fair, is to approach the process with an attitude that is professional, not antagonistic. Remember that courtesy and fairness from you will prompt those behaviors on the other end. It costs you nothing to be polite and may really improve the adjuster's feelings toward you.

This is not an invitation for the adjuster to walk all over you. The major thrust of this book is teaching you how to understand and carefully manage the process of homeowners insurance claims so that no one is able to take advantage of you.

To that end, let's discuss what to do when you and the adjuster do not agree.

How Good Is Your Insurance Adjuster?

Not all adjusters are created equal. Some claim adjusters work promptly to settle your claim with fairness. But of course, there are those who approach your claim strictly from the insurance company's viewpoint, considering only how to pay you as little as possible and delay you at every turn.

Using a bit of observation and common sense, you can get a feel for which type of adjuster is in charge of your claim. Look for these qualities as signs of a fair and qualified adjuster:

- Emotional self-control
- Effective communication
- Good time management
- Strong understanding of technology

- Good knowledge of your insurance policy
- Good understanding of repair procedures and costs

It is still possible to get the job done with a less-than-ideal adjuster, but you have to compensate for their shortcomings. For example, if your adjuster's communication skills are lacking, you should pay close attention to what they say, take good notes (or record everything), and ask a lot of follow-up questions to make certain everything is clear.

If you feel that your adjuster is using delaying tactics, keep track of exactly how many attempts you make to timely contact and continue your claim, and how your efforts are met. One exception to this rule: before making a snap judgment, consider whether your claim is one of hundreds in a certain area, such as after a powerful storm has damaged everybody's house for miles. The adjuster may simply be swamped by claims at the moment.

Problem: I disagree with the insurance adjuster.

The adjuster comes to look things over. He goes back to his office and uses computer software to calculate a number that tells you what he thinks your damage is worth – and it's far lower than you were expecting. Now what? Here are tips for making your case for a better settlement:

Understand Your Coverage

Before taking any further action, make sure you have reviewed your policy and have read all the fine print. Understand what your policy really does cover and to what extent. The Declaration Page of your insurance policy lists all the pertinent information; the pages that follow provide definitions and details.

Read your policy and pay attention to the phrasing. Make sure you know what you are entitled to and what you are not entitled to. One of the numerous hidden strategies used by property insurance claim adjusters is concealing coverage information in the hopes that you have not read your policy.

Being well-informed about your insurance policy is a sure-fire strategy to prevent falling victim to insurance adjuster tactics. Before entering any negotiation, it is usually a good idea to double-check your facts, so look over your policy thoroughly. If you understand your policy, you can also prevent unwittingly committing insurance fraud yourself.

If reviewing your policy reveals nothing about why your claim came out lower than you were expecting, the next step is to talk to your insurance company. You may ask for a **review of the insurance claim**, in which your insurance company will provide details of how they came to a specific number. This should give you a far better picture of where the discrepancy is occurring. It might even allow you to pinpoint an error on their part, which can be fixed.

Know Your Rights

Knowing how to deal with insurance adjusters includes understanding that you have the right to refuse their first offer. Remember, they work for the insurance company, so giving up as little information as possible is in their best interests – especially if they are trying to underpay on the value of your claim – but you paid for the policy and have the right to know the basis for their decisions and the information they used to come to that conclusion.

Short of hiring an attorney, letting an insurance adjuster know you are ready to negotiate and know your rights is one method to warn them off trying to bully you into a low settlement. Prepare a settlement amount that you believe you deserve if their initial offer is not fair. If you have evidence that their first offer should be higher, do not be afraid to challenge them. You can show them parts of your coverage and provide quotes from reputable contractors to back up your claim.

Consider a Public Adjuster (Or Just Get a Lawyer!)

Another option for protecting your rights is to engage a **public adjuster**. A public adjuster differs from a loss adjuster because they work for *you,* rather than the insurance company. They assist you in substantiating your claim and obtaining the best possible payment. If you choose this option, you will be responsible for paying their fee or compensating them in some other way for their services. A public adjuster is limited to what they can do and, unlike a lawyer, cannot compel an insurance company to respond to you through the judicial process.

Dispute the Decision

Contact the adjuster while remaining calm and polite. This does not mean you have to be a pushover, of course. You can state your case and make it clear that you are not satisfied with their estimate while keeping everything civil. As in most areas of life, people are much happier to work with someone who is level-headed and courteous.

In addition to or instead of calling, you should write a letter/email to the independent adjuster. In this letter, explain why you believe their settlement is not enough, and support your belief as thoroughly as possible with documents, contractor bids, photos, or anything else that is pertinent. The adjuster should respond within 10-to-14 days.

Document Everything

Any negotiation entails back-and-forth on the claim's main grounds. Keep any email exchanges. Take meticulous notes on your conversations or record the talks you have. A recorded statement for an insurance claim can aid in the resolution of disagreements. If you are going to record a conversation or take notes, make sure you tell the adjuster.

Make sure your final settlement offer fits the verbal promise by comparing it to your notes and recorded conversations.

Honest and cordial discussions with an insurance adjuster are the best way to get the most out of them. If you offend them, or if they lose faith in your honesty, you will not convince them to move on from their original offer. If you embellish or exaggerate the facts and discover insurance fraud, your claim may be denied, and you may face criminal prosecution.

When speaking to the claims adjuster, remember that there are certain things you should NOT say:

- Don't lie, embellish, exaggerate, or pad costs.
- Don't concede culpability or even partial responsibility for anything that happened.
- Don't speculate on the cause of the damages.

- Don't agree to make a recorded statement to them. Yes, you may record conversations with their permission – but if they ask for a recorded statement from you, say no.

An On-Site Inspection

If the letter and conversations with the claims adjuster did not help, you may request an on-site inspection. This is your opportunity to highlight your home's damage and show why it is more significant than what is stated in the adjuster's claims document.

Complain

If you have tried everything and the adjuster isn't budging, it is time to complain directly to the insurance company. You may proceed on your own, or you may hire an attorney. If I may say so, attorneys are well-practiced in complaining very convincingly on your behalf!

Call An Insurance Lawyer First

As you know, I am an insurance attorney. As such, my advice to you may come as no surprise – I recommend calling an experienced home insurance attorney before you ever make that first call to the insurance company. It is not because I want to boost my client list, either. Obviously, clients are my first consideration, and my business does not work without me advocating for them. But the truth is, I recommend contacting an insurance attorney first because I have seen what can happen when you *don't.*

- Our experience shows an 85-percent chance for your property damage claim to be underpaid by at least $10,000.

✧ Insurance companies (especially in Texas!) pay hundreds of millions of dollars each year lobbying for laws that are favorable to their bottom line – meaning that you, the consumer, are at a disadvantage when it comes to the fine points of arguing what you are entitled to.

✧ Insurance companies are huge corporate structures with layers of red tape, bureaucratic confusion, and forms filled with carefully crafted, confusing language. You are just one customer. Everything they have in place is to afford them a good chance of exhausting and demoralizing you if a dispute arises. They want you to accept what they offer and go away. Most people just do not have the will or the stamina to press the issue. They just want life to get back to normal, even if it means accepting less than they are entitled to. An insurance company may be counting on that.

What Can an Insurance Lawyer Do for You?

A good insurance lawyer can do a lot, as you will see from the list below. But the most immediate benefit of having an insurance attorney is the fact that he or she will deal directly with the insurance company on your behalf. You do not have to talk to the insurance company, argue your case, or take pages and pages of notes. That burden shifts to your lawyer, and your lawyer lives for this kind of thing.

And what else?

✧ An insurance lawyer can explain all the aspects of your policy and insurance law to you in language that makes sense.

✧ An insurance lawyer can navigate the claims process easily. They have been through this countless times before and know the steps and hurdles. The more complex your claim is, the more beneficial this service will be.

- An insurance lawyer knows what you are entitled to, so you won't end up leaving money on the table.
- If you get a claim denial, an insurance lawyer can tell you if that claim denial is valid, which at least can save you the time of pursuing a useless cause. Conversely, if the claim denial is *invalid*... that's when a lawyer becomes your best friend.
- A lawyer can file a Notice of Claim that complies with local laws.
- Lawyers are experts in negotiations. Are you? Do you want to bear the stresses of bargaining with a stubborn or reluctant company?
- Insurance lawyers have wide networks of experts in their field of practice, so they can obtain the services of those experts to support your claim, such as:
    - Contractors who can verify the extent of damages.
    - Meteorologists who can verify the weather patterns and systems to confirm that a storm was strong enough to damage your home.
    - Estimators who can generate evaluations of your losses.
    - Content experts who can verify the value of your personal property.
    - Insurance agents who can verify that your policy covers the losses claimed.

- ✧ Engineers to review the cause of your loss.

- ✧ A skilled property insurance lawyer can significantly increase the value of your claim.

Can I Afford to Hire a Lawyer?

Yes. What you cannot afford is to implicitly trust your insurance provider.

First, many lawyers offer free consultations. There is no cost or drawback to meeting with one to learn what they think about your claim.

In many cases, insurance lawyers operate on contingency agreements, meaning that they are only paid if and when *you* are paid. At that point, the attorney's fees come from the insurance company's payment to you. Typically, the attorney accepts a percentage of your settlement, and that percentage increases if the case must be taken to trial.

The more elaborate your claim is, and the more money that will be involved, the more useful an attorney will be. If something drastic does occur, even if the claim seems like a clear-cut case, an attorney is an excellent idea. Let's say that your home and its contents are destroyed in a fire. You are already under an enormous amount of stress, and there is a great deal of work to do to keep the claims process rolling, covering every aspect of returning your life to normal. An insurance lawyer will be your go-between and guardian to ensure that things are not missed, lost, or forgotten in the process. He or she will take care that the insurance company does not undercut the full extent of your damages. It is simple math: the more money your claim involves, the more money your insurance company can keep from you.

Finally, under Texas statute, if you win a court case against an insurance provider, the insurance agency is required to compensate your attorney's fees. That means the insurance company not only must pay you for your damages, but they also must pay your lawyer, who had to establish that fairness in court.

What the Law Requires of Insurance Companies

Insurance companies are regulated. There are procedural rules in place under the National Association of Insurance Commissioners (the NAIC) telling them what is required for a claim to be denied. So, if you file a claim for damages done by a storm, the insurance company cannot simply say, "No, we're not paying for that." They have to tell you, clearly and in writing, why you were not covered for that storm's damage, and the reasons they give have to line up with *your* insurance policy. It does not matter if 99-percent of policies don't cover storm damage of that type; if yours does, they cannot deny your claim.

Under the regulations, insurance companies:

- Cannot knowingly misrepresent the claimant's and insured's relevant facts or policy clauses relating to the coverage at issue.
- Must attempt in good faith to resolve promptly, lawfully, and fairly claims under which the responsibility has become reasonably clear.
- Cannot force insureds or their beneficiaries to institute suits to recover sums due under their policies by providing significantly less.

- Must deny claims *in writing* in whole or in part, providing the insured with a statement listing all bases for such rejection or denial, including the factual and legal justification for each reason. If their denial is based on a particular statute, applicable law or policy provision, condition or exclusion, the written denial shall contain a reference to it and clarify the application of the statute, applicable law or provision, condition, or exclusion to the claim.

This is fine in theory, but as is the case with many regulations, there are loopholes and definition problems. What does it mean to "knowingly" misrepresent relevant facts – maybe the misrepresentation was an accident! How much time does "promptly" mean – three weeks or three months? Just what does "clarify the application of the statute" mean – so that a judge can understand it, or so that a 10-year-old can? Depending on where you are and who is reviewing your case, the answers to these questions can be slippery indeed.

Some states have far more strict and precise penalties for unfair settlement practices, competition methods, or dishonest actions. For example, Florida's laws consider failure to provide the insured with a fair written description of the insurance policy basis, the facts or applicable law, to refuse a claim or propose a compromise settlement as unfair/dishonest. New York Law 3420(d)(2) includes written disclaimers (no rights reservations) in cases involving bodily injury and death; a failure to implement mandatory language into insurance contracts or obey statutory procedures can adversely affect a claim denial, resulting in significant statutory penalties against the insurer.

Unfortunately, insurance companies heavily lobby state legislatures in Texas. Therefore, the laws in Texas strongly favor those insurance companies.

To put it simply, varying state to state, insurance companies are able to get away with a lot of things. It is regrettable that in many cases, insurance companies "get away with it" because their customers don't question results, or they give up out of sheer frustration and exhaustion. A lawyer's job is to improve your chances against both the company and the frustration it can cause.

What Are "Good Faith" and "Bad Faith"?

When dealing with a legal dispute, the terms "good faith" and "bad faith" are used a lot. The legal meaning of these terms has to do with whether an interaction, negotiation or dispute is conducted honestly, and honorably, by both parties.

"Good faith" practices mean that both parties are following the same rules. They are working together toward a mutually beneficial decision. You want your claim settled fairly, and the insurance company wants its customers to know that they are a reliable company with integrity. However, operating in good faith does not mean that the insurance company must pay your claim; instead, if they deny your claim, they must have done so for a reason that is valid under the law and your policy. Even if the case goes all the way to trial, the insurance company can still be operating in good faith. You too must act in good faith, providing truthful and thorough information, even if it seems like that information might harm your case.

"Bad faith" practices usually mean that one, or both, of the parties has an ulterior motive or a hidden agenda. A bad faith argument will misrepresent the meaning of facts, statutes, regulations, or policies. Information may be withheld. Companies can get into trouble (including stiff fines and penalties, in addition to the bad press) for operating in bad faith, if that is discovered to be the truth. In the case of an insurance company, they might practice bad faith because they simply do not want to pay, or they might not want to set a precedent that they pay your type of claim. Thus, they obfuscate the facts and misrepresent the language of their policy. You, as the insured, could also be acting in bad faith if you are dishonest about the extent or cost of your damages.

When investigating a claim, an insurance provider must vigorously pursue proof supporting the claim of its insured. If it tries to discover only the facts that defeat the argument, it is operating in bad faith. Often unfair settlement practices may reach "bad faith" in the courtroom. It is a serious matter if an attorney can show that a company is operating in bad faith.

Processes For Settling and Resolving Claims

When Your Claim Is Undervalued

The first thing you must do is *realize* that your claim has been undervalued. Many people really do not know how much it costs to repair or replace something in their home (another reason why having a lawyer at this point can certainly help). If you have done the research and know that the offer is not good, you can negotiate with the adjuster.

Here is a simplified example of the negotiation process. You and the adjuster have reached an impasse. The adjuster offers $20,000 for your damages; you believe you are entitled to $27,000. You have written the letter and provided evidence that supports your claim.

The insurance company may look at your evidence and ignore it – $20,000 is the end of the conversation. Or they may say, "Fine, we don't completely agree, but we'll pay $22,000." At this point, you have the option of accepting their increased offer, counteroffering, or outright refusing. Refusal may feel satisfying, but it's not a great way to "play the game." Going to trial over a $5,000 difference is probably not worth the time or stress. If it seems like some bartering can be done, you might come back with a $24,000 counteroffer. If luck, grit, skill, and documentation are on your side, perhaps the company will meet you somewhere in the middle.

Negotiations are tricky, as you can see. If either party digs in their heels or refuses to budge, you must decide how far you want to go. Unless you have nerves of steel and a will of iron, it is probably a good idea to have a lawyer conducting negotiations for you. Hiring a lawyer signifies that you are serious about your claim; sometimes, the very act of hiring one will make an insurance company straighten up and get their act together.

Lawyers are trained for and have experience with the back-and-forth of negotiations. And despite the fact that your lawyer is certainly on your side, he or she also has a more objective viewpoint and a store of knowledge – meaning that your lawyer can tell you honestly whether that $22,000 from our example is really going to be the best you can do, or if the company can be coaxed up to a number closer to what you want. Your lawyer will certainly work hard to get that settlement offer improved – because what benefits you benefits your lawyer.

Eventually, having a professional lawyer conducting these talks can save you significant time and trouble.

When Your Claim Is Denied

If your insurance company denies your claim *verbally*, do not accept it, even if it sounds like they may be right. Insist on getting a *written denial.* The company is required by statute to provide one.

When you receive a written denial of your claim, the first thing you should do is confirm that denial clearly and sufficiently outlines the reason for rejection. A written denial that simply states, "You are not covered for this damage," is worthless and extremely inappropriate, just like a verbal denial.

A written denial should contain the following information:

1. The relevant policy language for this denial.

2. How the policy language works to exclude coverage.

Take care in reviewing this denial letter. Make certain that the relevant policy language is cited, but that it comes without extra, irrelevant detail about exclusions that have nothing to do with your claim. If it looks like your insurer has simply copied and pasted your policy into the letter, this is a sign that they are intentionally trying to confuse the matter. A longer letter full of big words does not signify that they are right.

While many written claim denials quote policy language, my experience is that often they do not make it sufficiently clear why or how that language relates to their denial. Perhaps they are intentionally trying to confuse you, or perhaps the person who wrote the letter simply did a bad job. Either way, if the claim denial is not clear, you have every right to ask questions and seek assistance.

Compare the language they cite to the language in your policy and make sure they have not left anything out, such as the final sentence of a paragraph that might actually cite an exception to the exclusion. Make certain that they are not misrepresenting the intent of the language in your policy. This is a tall order, and once more, an insurance lawyer is a valuable resource to assist with such a letter's review.

Ways in Which Insurance Companies Delay/Deny Claims

Insurance companies have a reputation for being tighter with their money than Ebenezer Scrooge. Despite the general rise in costs for insurance premiums, it is ironic how insurance providers dig deep to find a reason to deny you the coverage that you paid for. Below are some of the most common and creative ways that insurance companies may attempt to delay or deny your claim.

1. **They may claim negligence**. Claims of homeowner negligence are used quite often as a means of denying claims. Hypothetically speaking, let's say that you had a termite infestation in your home that you were meaning to have taken care of. Before you get the chance, however, a hurricane sweeps through your area and rips off a part of your roof. Even though the termites had nothing to do with the gale-force winds that tore apart your home, an insurance adjuster might find traces of

termites and claim that there was a pre-existing condition, resulting in a claim denial for negligence. As ludicrous as this sounds, it is entirely possible.

2. **Your allotted coverage is exceeded**. Insurance policies generally only cover liabilities up to a certain amount, meaning that if your damage exceeds this threshold, your insurance company may refuse to cover the difference or deny the claim entirely. For example, if your policy states that it will only cover up to $2,000 worth of damage to your collection of vintage guitars, but you claim $5,000 worth of damage, your insurance company may deny your claim for exceeding your coverage.
3. **Too many claims**. Commonly, denials result from submitting too many claims within a certain timeframe. Insurance companies make money betting on the likelihood that you will not have to use their service. When they must pay out too frequently, they incur losses. To combat this, try not to submit claims for minor incidents that you can pay for on your own. While incurring the cost yourself is less than ideal, it is much better than being faced with a claim denial for a major disaster for reasons of having too many claims.

What Is a "Reservation of Rights" Letter?

Insurers will sometimes send you a "Reservation of Rights" letter, or a combination "Declination and Reservation of Rights" letter. An explicit reservation of rights can include a complex and confusing declaration, such as:

"*We will continue to handle this claim even though a coverage question exists. However, no act of any company representative while investigating or negotiating the settlement of this claim or defending a lawsuit shall be construed as waiving any of our rights. We reserve the right, under the policy, to deny coverage to you or anyone claiming coverage under the policy. There may also be other reasons why coverage does not apply and we do not waive our right to deny coverage for any other valid reason which may arise."*

To break this down, they want to look more thoroughly at your claim, but don't want you thinking that their investigation means that you're covered. The reason they send such a letter is so that they can deny coverage later if they gather sufficient evidence to do so. It also means that they can reject claims on other contractual grounds, and not just those in the original declination letter.

Note that a Reservation of Rights does not absolutely mean your claim will be denied – but it is not a good sign. Your claim has something about it that makes the company think they may be able to deny or partially deny coverage. A Reservation of Rights can sometimes be used improperly, like as a delay tactic or a way to worry you into taking a much smaller settlement because you are afraid the whole claim will be denied.

A Declination and Reservation of Rights letter combines the two functions of a claim denial (or partial claim denial) plus a Reservation of Rights saying that the insurance company is denying all or part of your claim but still investigating.

Should you receive such a letter, I recommend that you review the letter and your policy carefully. The letter should contain specific information about any part of your claim that may not be covered.

Insurance companies are not allowed to carry on a Reservation of Rights indefinitely or conduct an "investigation" for months on end. This is another reason why consulting an insurance attorney is such a good idea.

Is It Worth Going to Trial?

Only a small fraction of insurance cases are litigated to final judgment where they are taken to court and tried before a judge or jury. Usually, neither party really wants to go this route on an insurance coverage matter.

For you, it is a lengthy process to take a case to trial. Do not let what you have seen on TV convince you that anything happens quickly – it can take years to get a case through the litigation process.

For the insurance company, going to trial is costly, and it can set precedents they do not want the public to see. Moreover, courts are fallible. Definitions and protections can change from state to state or even courtroom to courtroom, depending on interpretation of the language.

Most of the time, claims are settled without going to trial, through negotiation between the parties. This is usually the fastest and simplest solution for everyone involved – including you.

However, there are instances when cases simply cannot be negotiated. Maybe the statutes are unclear. Maybe no one agrees on the policy's interpretation. Maybe the parties can't reach a settlement offer. Maybe the insurance company is truly operating in bad faith – and something has to give.

When coverage cases go to trial, they can be before a judge alone or before a jury.

Declaratory Decisions

Declaratory decisions happen when a case is litigated before a judge only, without getting a jury involved. The judge interprets the law and/or language of the policy as it relates to the law. This type of litigation is most common when facts are at the core of a coverage dispute. If the dispute depends solely on the interpretation of the language in a policy form, either party can request a declaratory judgment and, if necessary, an appeal of that decision.

In a declaratory judgment action, the insurer or insured can bring the coverage dispute to the jurisdictional court, asking the court to determine the coverage issue and each party's rights under the contract. The court typically responds in one of three ways:

- The judge relieves the insurer if coverage does not exist.
- The judge guides the insurer to pay or protect whatever coverage exists.
- The judge determines that the case must go to jury trial to determine whether coverage occurs based on the case's circumstances and characteristics.

What are the considerations of relying on a declaratory decision? Here are some things you need to know. These are not "pros" and "cons" because each of these details can really work for or against you when a judge is only making the decision.

1. Both parties know who is trying the case ahead of time. This makes it possible for attorneys to research a judge's past decisions and predisposition, to see how best to present the case. In fact, the predisposition of a judge can sometimes make an attorney move for a jury trial, rather than taking chances before a judge who is known to favor the other side.

2. Judges *generally* (it's not a guarantee!) are well-educated and have read a great deal of law, allowing them to understand the complex language of an insurance policy.

3. Judges are less likely to fall for a bad faith argument – if your insurance company truly has no ground to stand on or is being purposely difficult or even dishonest, a judge will probably spot it easily. The judge's reaction, however, depends on how sympathetic he or she is to the insurance company.

4. Decisions on appeal are more likely to be overturned if it was a lone judge's decision, rather than a jury decision. Courts of appeal (called Appellate Courts) prefer to leave jury verdicts alone; they don't mind as much when overturning the opinion of a fellow judge.

Jury Trial

Some coverage cases do eventually go to trial. If things have gotten this far, you may feel like your insurance company deserves to be sued in court. Whether or not you get any money at all, it's the principle of the matter that counts now, and you want to drag them in front of a jury and let the world know what they did to you. This is a natural feeling, especially if you are convinced that your insurance company is operating in bad faith. That being said, listen to the advice of your attorney. We all want justice to be done, but a trial's outcome is never certain, no matter how right you believe you are.

Insurance coverage cases are civil cases, rather than criminal cases. Civil cases cover all matters where no crime was committed: personal injury, workers compensation, malpractice, family court, and divorce court are just a few examples of matters addressed by civil law. If you take your insurance company to trial, you are the "plaintiff" or the "complainant," and in this role, you file a complaint against the insurance company, which is the "defendant".

For our purposes, there are two main differences between criminal trials and civil trials:

The Burden of Proof. In criminal cases, it is the duty of the prosecution to prove the guilt of the accused "beyond a reasonable doubt." Civil cases are not held to that standard of proof because no one's civil liberties are at stake (i.e., no one is going to prison over this). The burden of proof in a civil case must convince the judge/jury that *it is more likely than not that the defendant* (your insurance company) *committed the act of which they are accused* (denying part or all of your claim when they had no right to do so). That sounds promising for you, but it is hard to tell which way a jury is going to interpret evidence.

Jury Consensus. In a criminal case, juries must vote unanimously. However, in civil cases, it is only necessary that a majority of the jury agree. Some states require only nine of the twelve jurors to agree. In Texas, 10 of the 12 (or 5/6th of the jury) must agree on a verdict.

Taking an insurance coverage case to trial has its pros and cons. So, here they are. I will give you the bad news first.

The CONS – not deal-breakers, but things you should know:

1. I already mentioned the biggest con for you, which is the sheer amount of time it takes to get a matter to trial. Your presence will be necessary for depositions, the court case itself, and testimonies.
2. There is no certainty as to who will end up on your jury.
3. Insurance coverage is complicated and *boring*. Not many people enjoy being on jury duty anyway; now they have to listen to a couple lawyers argue about insurance definitions and exclusions. It is quite difficult to keep a jury's attention on these matters.

The PROS – not guaranteed, but things that might help:

1. Chances are good that most of your jury has insurance policies of their own (one or more of home, auto, or health insurance), so they understand the expense of insurance and what one expects from a policy.
2. These same policy owners understand the headache of dealing with irritating, complicated policies and legalese. In a court case, there is a legal presumption that you, the plaintiff, read and understood your insurance policy when you bought it. But the truth is, almost everyone on that jury is thinking, "I've never read or understood a full insurance policy in my life."They sympathize with where you are coming from.
3. Most policy owners at some point have had to file an insurance claim, and filing a claim seldom means anything good has happened. Jurors can identify with what it is like to need help with their insurance company.

Conclusion

If there is one lesson I hope you take from this chapter; it is that getting expert help from an insurance lawyer to assist in an insurance claim has many important advantages. You do not have to settle for less than what you deserve or accept the word of your insurance company simply because they are bigger than you. It is your right to ensure that you get what you deserve from the policy you paid for with hard-earned money.

CHAPTER EIGHT

WHAT IF MY POLICY IS CANCELLED?

There are many reasons why your homeowners insurance policy might be cancelled and many reasons why you don't want that to happen! Whether or not those reasons are your fault, it is important that you move quickly to obtain a new policy as soon as possible. Cancellation of your policy puts you at risk of huge expenses if your home is damaged. Without a policy, you must pay out-of-pocket for any damages that occur to your home or property.

If you have a mortgage, keeping active homeowners insurance is almost certainly part of your mortgage agreement. If your insurance is cancelled, you might be considered as defaulting on the loan, or your insurance company might instate **force-placed coverage** at your expense – which is very expensive, indeed. Force-placed insurance is also known as creditor-placed or lender-placed insurance. It is exactly what it sounds like: if you let your homeowners insurance policy lapse, your lender "forces" another policy in its place because your lender has a vested interest in your property's value. You should avoid this, if at all possible. Not only is the cost high, but because your lender cares only about the real property, these policies have poor coverage for your personal property.

Reasons for Cancellation

The ease of obtaining a replacement policy really depends on why your insurance company stopped your policy in the first place. If the reasons were outside of your control, for example, due to a change inside the insurance company itself, then other insurance companies should not have a problem working with you. Policy cancellations that are your fault due to missed payments – or worse – fraudulent claims, will make it much harder and more expensive for you to find new insurance.

After you have had a policy for longer than 60 days, the reasons that a policy can be *cancelled* are fairly limited. State statutes vary, but your insurance company cannot simply cancel your policy on a whim. Cancellation means that *you* have done something violating your policy terms, or at least your insurance company has reason to believe that you have. In Texas, the reasons that your insurance company can cancel are:

1. You committed fraud in obtaining the coverage or submitting a claim.
2. You have failed to pay premiums when they are due.
3. Continuation of the policy would result in a violation of business or insurance law.

Reasons for cancellation within the initial 60 days of the policy are broader, because it can occur because of unintentional miscalculations or misunderstandings on the part of either party. This is why the insurance company must give you their reasons for cancellation in writing, so you can submit this as evidence to another insurance company that you were not responsible for the cancellation.

The logic is simple enough here: cancellation that occurs after a policy is 60 days old strongly implies that you were in the wrong.

Making timely payments is your responsibility. Many mortgage companies permit annual insurance premiums to be tied in with monthly mortgage payments, which can be helpful depending on how reliable you are about making those payments. As long as you pay your mortgage each month, your insurance policy will remain in force. But missing a mortgage payment means double the trouble because you have compromised your insurance coverage as well as your mortgage loan.

I previously mentioned CLUE, the Comprehensive Loss Underwriting Exchange database, on which all insurance companies can see if you had a policy that was cancelled without renewal and the reason why.There's no hiding your insurance history! To avoid problems like this, it is simply best to make your payments on time and deal with your insurance company honestly.

Reasons for Non-Renewal

More often than cancellation, policies are simply not renewed when the premium period is over, if the insurance company has an issue with your coverage that is not directly related to your own wrongdoing. Most homeowners insurance policies renew annually, so in the case of non-renewal, they notify you that your policy will cease at the end of the term.

There are a number of reasons why a home insurance company might not renew your policy at the end of the term, such as:

1. **You have filed too many claims.** The more claims you file, the more you look like an insurance risk. If you have made too many of a particular type of claim – such as dog bites, or fire/water damage – these are red flags to the insurance company. To prevent this, conduct regular maintenance and upkeep on your home and pay for small repairs out of pocket.

2. **Your risk level has risen dramatically.** Sometimes, there is a change in circumstances that puts your home in a higher-risk category. For example, geography and weather patterns can change, putting your home in a flood, hurricane, or wildfire risk zone. Risk levels also rise if you install certain items (pools, trampolines) or make certain alterations to your home.

3. **Your credit score is bad / you have a criminal record.** Both factors increase your risk in the insurance company's eyes: they see you as less likely to pay your bills and more likely to commit fraudulent behavior.

4. **You have obtained aggressive pets / dogs on the restricted breed list.** The parameters of this guideline change state-by-state. Whether or not it seems fair, some insurance companies refuse to cover homeowners with a particular breed of dog (bully-breeds are particularly notorious, but they are not the only breed on the list). Check with your insurance company to be certain if your pet's breed is a problem. Occasionally, exceptions are made for dogs with obedience training certificates. And, regardless of the breed, a dog with a history of biting will make your insurance company far more likely to drop your policy.

5. **Your relationship with the home has changed.** Perhaps you have stopped inhabiting the home, or you have started a home-based business there. In cases like these, different types of insurance coverages are required.

6. **Changes inside the insurance company.** The company may no longer provide homeowners coverage, discontinue that line of insurance, or cease operations in your state. Of course, this reason is not your fault... unless you were on the Board of Directors that made the decision.

My Homeowners Insurance Is Stopping – What Now?

Your insurance company must inform you when they are going to cancel your policy, giving you a window of 10-to-20 days to obtain new insurance, depending on your state. **In Texas, statutes require that notification of cancellation must take 10 days before cancellation.**

Non-renewal notice is required to be at least 45 days – and in some states, it is almost twice that much – and your insurance company must send you a letter explaining their non-renewal decision. **Texas statutes require that you be notified 60 days prior to non-renewal.**

Most states have consumer laws in place that dictate when an insurance can raise your premiums or refuse to renew your coverage due to a claim. Some jurisdictions, for example, prohibit insurance companies from boosting your rates after your first claim or any claim that does not result in compensation (also known as zero-dollar claims).

Some states prohibit insurance companies from citing weather or natural disasters as a rationale for not renewing their contracts. To learn more about state-specific consumer protection and other insurance information, contact your state's insurance department.

In the event your policy is cancelled or not renewed, you may do the following:

1. **If you don't understand why the cancellation/ non-renewal happened, ask**. Contact your insurance company and find out what the problem is and how you could have prevented it. Insurance companies may be willing to refer you to an affiliate company. If you can correct the problem in a timely way, they may even be willing to keep insuring you.

2. **You have the right to appeal a non-renewal decision.** Explain to your insurance provider why you believe the non-renewal was unjust. Winning this appeal usually requires demonstrating that your home isn't as dangerous as the insurer believes. Perhaps climatic risks vary significantly within a limited geographical area in your state. Thus, risk exposure varies from block to block. You might be able to get your insurance back if you can show this. You can also indicate that you have reduced your risk exposure by replacing the roof or making other improvements that reduce your vulnerability to significant hazards.

3. **Explore your options using Insurify.** At this site, you can compare homeowners insurance quotes from various companies. If non-renewal was for a reason outside of your control, you may even find a better rate than you were paying before.

4. **Contact your state's insurance department**. Not only can they recommend highly-rated insurance companies, but if you're in an unusual situation that caused

your policy's non-renewal, they might be able to direct you to a company that can help.

5. **Contact your state's Fair Access to Insurance Requirements (FAIR) Plan**. If you are really having trouble finding insurance coverage, most states have a FAIR Plan, a high-risk insurance pool run by the state's insurance administration and paid by private businesses. Each state has its own set of approval criteria. Some of them demand you to show that at least three insurance companies have rejected you before applying for a FAIR Plan. These last-resort plans likewise have tight limitations that private insurance does not have. They usually don't include liability coverage or supplementary valuables coverage, and personal property is usually just protected for its real monetary value. In Texas, the website for the FAIR plan is https://www.texasfairplan.org/.

Summary

The cancellation or non-renewal of your homeowners insurance policy means you will have to take steps in a timely manner to ensure that your coverage continues. The easiest way to avoid cancellation is simply to be a good consumer. Behave with integrity in your claim filings and pay your premiums on time.

An insurance company's decision for non-renewal may be appealed, but if the non-renewal is for a reason outside of your control, is not necessarily a bad thing. You have many options and may even find that you can obtain insurance for less cost than before.

The most important thing in either case is that your home and possessions remain protected from the unexpected, so don't delay replacing your policy!

CONCLUSION

Congratulations! Together we have made it through the entire insurance process! I hope that this guide has been of assistance in navigating the process of insuring your home.

As we conclude, I offer the following reminders that I consider that most important aspects of everything we have covered here:

1. **If your home is not insured, correct that right away! (See Chapters One, Two, and Eight)** There really is no good excuse to go without homeowners insurance. I understand that insurance is an expense that does not always seem necessary... That feels true until the moment you need it. And when you need it, you *really* need it. Don't risk your home's value or your life savings by neglecting this important piece of financial responsibility.

2. **Know what is in your homeowners insurance policy (See Chapters Three and Four).** Unfortunately, insurance policies are not thrilling page-turners. But you need to be aware of your exclusions and policy limits. The Declarations Page provides a convenient summary of coverage. Still, reading the "fine print" is always a good idea.

3. **Review your policy, as necessary. (See Chapters Three and Four)** If there are changes in your life, changes in your property, new acquisitions, or just the passage of time, make certain that your homeowner's insurance policy is still as good as it needs to be. What seemed like a solid policy many years ago may no longer be sufficient, or necessary. When you receive your annual renewal from the insurance company, this is a good time to check over your policy limits and coverage to decide if you are still protected.

4. **Make a thorough inventory of your possessions and their values (See Chapter Four).** This is a little bit like hitting the gym every day or putting money aside instead of enjoying a vacation – it is not a lot of fun to do in the present, but oh boy, in the future, you will be so glad you did! Besides, technology is really on your side here. There are apps available now to make the process more streamlined. Making a video record with your phone is a snap. If you are ever in the position where you have to account for some or all of your possessions to get them replaced, you're going to thank your lucky stars you made the effort.

5. **Remember that the insurance company is in business to make money (See Chapters Five, Six and Seven).** Your insurance company will hopefully deal with you fairly and honestly. Even so, insurance companies have shareholders and Boards of Directors who are looking at the bottom line, and they do not increase their profits by paying claims. As long as you are making payments, they'll love you. The moment you need to file a claim, they are looking for reasons to deny. Be vigilant

and stick up for your rights. You do not have to "take their word" for claim values or denials.

6. **Seek the help of a professional (See Chapter Seven).** You have the right to get help if and when your homeowners insurance policy/company becomes confusing, confounding, or downright confrontational. You owe it to yourself and your investment to be certain that you are getting the best deal possible within your policy's boundaries. You have done your part. Reaching out to a professional insurance attorney ensures that your insurance company does its part as well.

Your home is probably your most valuable possession as well as your biggest financial investment, with the best likelihood of paying off in the future. Making certain that your home retains its value, even after a disaster, is the entire financial point of an insurance policy.

But more than that, our homes serve as a refuge and sanctuary from the world's pressures. As the old saying goes, "Home is where the heart is." Those old sayings stick around for a reason! A home is so much more than a building in which you sleep: it is the centerpiece of your life. Protecting your home and everything it contains is an essential precaution. If the unexpected ever happens, a good insurance policy and the good advice of an insurance professional are the best ways to get your home, and your life, back to normal. Protect yourself, your home, and your family so you can rest easy.

GLOSSARY OF TERMS

Some of the terms used in an insurance policy might sound like secret code patched together by a team of lawyers. Here I offer a list of many common terms in homeowners insurance, and simple definitions for what these words mean *in the context of this book.*

Please note that for questions you may have about *legal definitions* for insurance and other terms below, consult your policy, your insurance agent, and/or an insurance attorney.

Actual Cash Value: This is the current value of your house and belongings, or their value at the time of the loss, and *not* their value at the time of purchase.

Adjuster: an individual working for the insurance company whose job it is to investigate, negotiate and resolve an insurance claim.

"Bad Faith" Practices: when one or both of the parties in a dispute have an ulterior motive or a hidden agenda, and manipulate their case by withholding information, misrepresenting facts, etc.

Basic Coverage:The minimum level of property insurance which protects against fire, theft, and vandalism.

Bid: The amount of money a contractor requests in exchange for repairing/rebuilding all or part of your home.

Blanket Policy: This means that all of your personal property is all covered by the same insurance amount.

Broad Form Coverage: A level of insurance better than basic coverage, extended to include a number of additional named perils.

Claimant: The person(s) filing an insurance claim

Contingency Agreement/Fees: An agreement with an attorney that he/she will only be paid if and when his/her client's claim is successful.

Declaratory Decisions: These are the results of a case litigated before a judge only, without a jury. This type of litigation is most common when facts are at the core of a coverage dispute.

Declination and Reservation of Rights Letter: a letter sent by an insurance company stating that they are declining part of a claim, and investigating the remainder of the claim, but that their investigation does not mean that they consider any part of the claim valid.

Deductible: This is the portion of the damages that you must contribute for the insurance company to pay the rest. If you have damages of $10,000 and a $500 deductible, you will receive $9,500 from the insurance company for a claim on those damages. That first $500 is on you. Agreeing to larger deductibles usually lowers the costs of insurance premiums.

Dwelling: This is your home and the structures attached to it (decks, porches, garages, etc.). Buildings not attached to the house, including separate garages, are given coverage (usually limited) under a different part of the insurance policy.

Endorsements: An option for increased liability coverage. Endorsements allow you to increase liability limits beyond what is ordinary.

Estimate: The amount of money that an appraiser believes will be required to repair/replace your damaged home.

Exclusion: a loss that is not covered by your homeowners insurance policy

Extended Replacement Cost Policy: This is a comprehensive policy that pays for replacement of your home's structure, even if that replacement cost exceeds your policy limits. Extended Replacement Cost has a cap at 20-to-25-percent higher than policy limits.

Force-placed Coverage: Also known as creditor-placed or lender-placed insurance, this is a policy your lender "forces" into the place of a lapsed insurance policy.

"Good Faith" Practices: when both parties in a dispute are following the same rules, which are valid under the law and the insurance policy in question.

Guaranteed Replacement Cost Policy: This is a comprehensive policy that pays for replacement of your home's structure, even if that replacement cost exceeds your policy limits. Guaranteed Replacement Costs have no cap limit and are more expensive policies.

Hazard: something that increases the chances that a peril will happen and increases the likelihood of a loss.

Independent Adjuster: an adjuster hired by the insurance company from a third party.

Liability Coverage: Your policy provides some coverage for damages and medical bills if you are held responsible for accidentally causing physical harm to another person or their property.

Loss: the damage that your property suffers as the result of a peril.

Named Insured: This is probably you – that's why you picked up the book, right? The named insured is responsible for the homeowners insurance policy and the dwelling it covers, and in most cases, the named insured must be living in that dwelling.

Named-peril Policy: an insurance policy in which you are covered only for the perils listed in your policy.

Non-renewal: When an insurance company elects not to continue an insurance policy after the policy term (usually a year, for homeowners policies) is over.

Open-peril Policy: an insurance policy in which you are covered *unless* a specific peril is excluded in your policy.

Owner: The owner is the person or entity (such as a trust) whose name is on the most recently recorded deed to the property.

Peril: An event that could cause damage your home or your possessions.

Personal Property: These are the things that you own (clothing, furniture, electronics) that are not part of the house.

Premium: This is the cost of insurance. For homeowners policies, premiums usually come in one-year terms.

Public Adjuster: a professional who can be hired by a claimant. A public adjuster's job is to help substantiate an insurance claim and obtain the best possible payment from the insurance company.

Replacement Cost: A replacement-cost policy covers the actual cash value of your home, *without* taking depreciation into consideration.

Reservation of Rights Letter: a letter sent by an insurance company stating that they are investigating a claim, but that their investigation does not mean that they consider the claim valid.

Scope / Scope of Work (SOW) – an agreement about the work that needs to be performed to repair/replace damage. This contains a timeline, milestones, deliverables, reports, and a description of the end product that is expected.

Special Coverage: This is the name for the highest level of property protection, a policy which operates on an open-peril basis.

Written Denial: insurance companies denying a claim must provide a report stating the reasons for the denial and pointing out the relevant portions of the policy as well as applicable insurance laws or statutes.

ABOUT ME:

Greetings! I'm Eric Dick, a dedicated and passionate Houston native who believes in the transformative power of resilience and education. I am eternally thankful to Houston for instilling the invaluable lesson that we must never abandon our dreams, no matter how challenging our circumstances.

My humble beginnings trace back to my twenties when I diligently worked as a Papa John's pizza delivery driver—those days of hard work, perseverance, and sheer willpower allowed me to dream bigger and foster an unwavering faith in my capabilities. Today, I stand proudly as the owner of Dick Law Firm, a testament to my relentless spirit and dedication.

The journey from delivering pizzas to owning a law firm is undeniably challenging, yet the enriching life experiences in between have significantly contributed to my personal and professional growth. One such impactful experience was when I began working in the insurance sector under the guidance of my grandmother, Gene Dick, a trailblazer in her own right. She was the first female insurance agent for American General in Houston, Texas, during the 1960s. Learning the ropes from her not only taught me a deep understanding of the insurance industry but also instilled the values of tenacity and professionalism.

At Dick Law Firm, we've had the privilege to serve thousands of Houston consumers, primarily with home insurance claims. These typically revolve around windstorm damage claims for properties insured by companies like Allstate. Our work provides peace of mind to our clients in times of great stress, reinforcing our commitment to the community.

I am an ardent advocate of continuous learning and personal growth, which led me to complete an MBA from Rice University amidst the global upheaval caused by the COVID-19 pandemic. This accomplishment is a stark reminder that obstacles are opportunities in disguise if one is willing to seek them.

As a firm believer in the adage "to whom much is given, much is expected," I take my responsibility towards giving back to the community seriously. In line with this belief, I was elected as a trustee for the Harris County Department of Education, and I am honored to have served as its President. During my tenure, we initiated significant projects such as Texas's first public recovery high school and a program that assists teachers with school supplies expenses. These initiatives resonate with my commitment to creating a supportive environment for educators and students.

Being a proud Texan, I have channeled my love for my home state into the pages of a book about Texas history. Through this endeavor, I hope to share the vibrant culture, traditions, and historical events that make Texas unique.

I am blessed to share my life with my wonderful wife, Danielle, and our three precious children – two beautiful daughters and a son. They are the driving force behind my passion to create a better future for our family and the community we proudly call home.

In conclusion, my story is about resilience, hard work, and a commitment to serving the community. As I look toward the future, I remain dedicated to leveraging my experiences and skills to make a significant difference in the lives of the people around me. Houston has taught me never to give up, and I intend to continue honoring this lesson through my work and personal life.

For more information about Eric and his practice, please visit:

www.DickLawFirm.com

For speaking requests or other inquiries, please phone 888-660-0088x700 or email **Eric@DickLawFirm.com**.